# Vegetarian Sushi Secrets

## 101 HEALTHY AND DELICIOUS RECIPES

### MARISA BAGGETT

TUTTLE Publishing

Tokyo | Rutland, Vermont | Singapore

# Contents

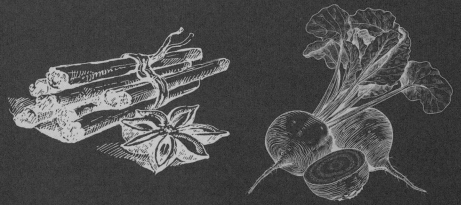

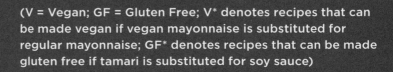

## Inside-Out Rolls

## Hand Rolls

## Desserts & Drinks

## Index 126
## Acknowledgment 128

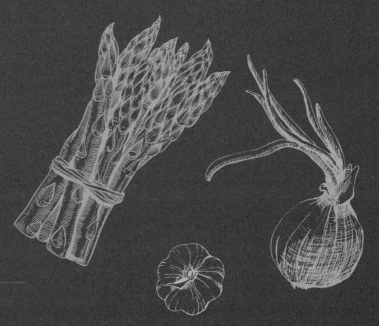

# Try This at Home!

## Foreword by Justin Fox Burks and Amy Lawrence

**S**o there we were, tucked away in a dark corner of a Japanese restaurant one night in Memphis. We were out of our depth.

First, we stumbled over the pronunciation of "edamame." Then, we ate the *entire* bowl of soybeans—pods and all. After searching in vain for discarded pods, our server kindly set us straight. We had much to learn.

Strangely enough for Southern vegetarians, sushi is a significant part of our diet. We grew up around Memphis and stayed in the area for college. Sushi dates were an escape from cafeteria food. It became a tradition for both special occasions and bad-day pick-me-ups.

In time, we moved out of the shadows and sidled up to the sushi bar, where we could watch the chefs assemble their beautiful works of art. We asked questions—lots of them.

Our intense enthusiasm led us to find our favorites and develop preferences. We picked up the terminology, and could soon say the words with confidence (and a big Southern accent). But sushi was still only for special occasions.

One Valentine's Day about twelve years ago, we worked up the courage to try to make vegetarian sushi at home. Some light research plus the foggy recollections of interrogating long-suffering sushi chefs years ago led us to cautiously believe that we were up to the task. After all, we were no slouches in the kitchen!

We remember the excitement of that trip to the Asian grocery to pick up all the tools and ingredients we needed to make our very first vegetarian sushi rolls. We arrived home with the items, laid everything out on the counter, and got to work.

Trepidation built as we started the sushi rice, sliced vegetables and decided which ingredients we wanted to pair together. But all of the anxiety melted away when our first roll stayed together and looked just about right. It may not have been perfect—or all that pretty—but this first tentative bloom of success was the next thrilling step in our lifelong sushi journey. The first bite tasted like victory.

These days, sushi is missing the rarity and mystery it had when we first tried it. We still enlist sushi to celebrate life's high points, but now we also have it for lunch on a Saturday or dinner on a Tuesday. And it's the perfect thing to make when you have guests coming over.

If they don't know any better, diners may come to the conclusion that sushi consists solely of a piece of raw fish and a little rice. The reality is that sushi is infinitely adaptable to a vegetarian diet. We love to add unexpected seasonal elements like pickled okra, sweet potatoes, and corn, as well as other local ingredients.

*Vegetarian Sushi Secrets* is truly a gift—it places a lifetime of sushi knowledge into your hands. It's not about what's missing; it's about tapping into a vast array of fruits and vegetables, pairing favorite flavors, and finding new combinations that will delight your senses. It's also about adding a healthy focus to our diets. It will open your mind and expand your palate. Use it as a road map for your next special meal.

**Justin Fox Burks** and **Amy Lawrence**
authors of *The Southern Vegetarian* and
*The Chubby Vegetarian* blog

# A Passion for Sushi

## Foreword by Allison Day

Sushi has been a part of my life as long as I can remember. My family's New Year's Day tradition involved driving to the local Japanese restaurant to pick up a big order of sushi. For many years, this was the entire extent of my sushi experience.

Later, I started to slowly branch out with my sushi eating. The man I would go on to marry came up with the idea that I should start a food blog—all about sushi.

Because I was a college student on a budget, a restaurant review blog was out of the question. I decided to first teach my readers how to make sushi, and then come up with all sorts of creative recipes for sushi. It was through this mutual passion for less traditional takes on sushi that Marisa and I found each other several years ago.

With all this sushi making at home, it wasn't long before I took over my family's New Year's sushi duty, making dozens of different rolls every New Year's morning. Sushi became my go-to contribution to potlucks, which led to experimentation in meat- and fish-free rolls for my vegetarian friends. I've added tempura-fried and grilled vegetables to maki rolls, topped inari sushi with mushrooms, and even made a roll with hummus and bell peppers. While most people may automatically associate sushi with raw fish, I've found it to be an excellent format for vegetable-based rolls as well.

Over the years, all this sushi-making led to an interest in developing sushi recipes that even the most sushi-averse would enjoy, as well as a passion for sustainability in sushi. These interests are two very big reasons why I'm so excited for *Vegetarian Sushi Secrets*. Marisa and I share a passion for feeding people and showing them just how delicious sushi can be. And what better way to promote sustainability than to prove that sushi can be crave-worthy even in the absence of fish?

To have an entire cookbook full of delicious vegetarian options is beyond exciting for me. At first glance, I'm already making a mental list of all the recipes I want to try, and then introduce to my vegetarian friends.

If you're new to sushi, the inari and nigiri section (page 58) is a great place to start. In Japan, inari is the kids' meal of sushi, which means it's great for beginners. (And to be honest, many people—including myself—remain big fans of inari sushi well into adulthood!) As for nigiri, it's simply a ball of rice topped with something—in this case, vegetables or a slice of Japanese-style omelette. If you're hesitant about the seaweed aspect, as many people are, this is a great way to ease yourself into the world of sushi.

For those more familiar with Americanized sushi rolls, Marisa has created tasty vegetarian versions of all your favorites. From Spider Rolls made with mushrooms to Dynamite Rolls with tofu, to Caterpillar Rolls with her Vegetarian Eel Sauce, and even a vegetarian version of the classic California Roll, the best-known American takes on sushi make a great vegetarian showing in this cookbook.

One of the things I love most about Marisa, as evidenced beautifully by both of her cookbooks, is that she isn't afraid to get creative with sushi while still staying true to the traditional techniques and spirit. Whether you're strictly vegan, wanting to eat more sustainably, or just trying to get more vegetables in your life, there's something for everyone in this cookbook!

Allison Day
author of *Sushi Day* blog

# My Life with Sushi
## How I Become a Sushi Chef

It always begins with the same question: Why sushi? My relationship with sushi began in the invincibility phase of my early twenties. Even though I was fortunate to own and operate a restaurant, catering company and coffeehouse, I was suffering a significant case of career wanderlust. I knew something was missing and I felt that I wasn't "there" yet. To help with that inner nagging and keep me on my toes, my businesses offered so many food services that I was forced to be creative. At that time, you could call the Chocolate Giraffe and ask me to consider crafting a custom menu or experience. In a small Mississippi college town with limited options, this was a great source of fun. It was inconsistent. Problematic. But it answered my need for variety.

I can recall that fateful day when a local orthodontist asked to reserve the entire space for a private party. I was excited, but I was also beside myself because the request was for a sushi party. I nodded with enthusiasm as I recorded requests for items like miso soup, seaweed salad, spicy tuna, crunchy shrimp, and all manner of exotic things I had never heard of, much less attempted to create. I wanted to cry. Yet I stayed cool on the outside under the weight of fear and the stares of disbelief from my employees.

As soon as the session was over, I flipped out. I had promised to create an experience built around something I had never once seen or tasted in person. I had no way to run out to my local sushi bar and have a sushi experience, because there wasn't one in town. The nearest place was several hours away, and I didn't have the time to make the journey. For the first time, I wondered if I had bitten off way more than I could chew.

Armed with my library card, I ventured down the street to the public library and checked out as many books on Japan and Japanese cuisine as I was allowed. Much to my dismay, there were very few sources that spent significant time on the subject of sushi. (Blogs and informative websites were not a thing just yet.) What little information I did find I studied intensively. I became a little more comfortable with the idea.

The next hurdle was trying to locate the exotic ingredients. My local Asian market had some of the basics—rice, soy sauce and rice vinegar. But where was I supposed to get sushi-grade tuna, *katsuobushi* (smoked fish used to make basic Japanese soup stock), or *shichimi togarashi* (Japanese seven-flavored pepper blend)? The necessary equipment was also a problem. Even if I could find them, could I justify to my business partners (aka Mom and Dad) the need for carbon-steel knives, a *hangiri* (the flat-bottomed bowl with straight sides made of cypress used only for

Tofu and Avocado Caterpillar Rolls (page 97)

The author enjoying sushi with friends

marinating sushi rice), a *shamoji* (the wooden paddle used only for tossing steamed sushi rice with the dressing), and a large rice cooker just for this one party? I knew better than to even ask.

I had to improvise with my ingredients as well as with the tools I needed to make the sushi. My staff and I spent an incredible amount of energy perfecting a cold smoker for salmon and figuring out how many bricks and cans were needed to weigh down the lid of a pot to cook rice on the stove. When we couldn't source suggested ingredients like pickled eggplant, we used what we felt were suitable substitutions—like the local staple, pickled okra.

Somehow we made it work. The party was a success. And that should have been enough. But when people found out that the Chocolate Giraffe served sushi (just that once), the requests for more kept coming in. Naturally, I promised we would start having sushi nights once a month. That turned into once every two weeks, then once a week, and then finally a small portion of the regular restaurant menu was dedicated to sushi. We were the talk of the town!

I couldn't believe how much people loved our sushi. One day, I received a long-distance call with reservations for twelve! The man on the phone sounded so excited to bring his out-of-town colleagues to Starkville, more than an hour's drive, for a sushi experience. We prepared and waited anxiously for them to arrive. But the moment the businessman from one of Mississippi's car manufacturing plants arrived with his eleven male colleagues from Japan, I went to the restroom, locked myself in, and cried. I knew my sushi was far from authentic, and I finally decided that I was no longer an invincible "sushi chef" who would remain beloved and sheltered in my small Mississippi hometown. My staff knocked on the door and tried to lure me out. They threatened to call my parents. I eventually emerged to face the situation that I had wholeheartedly gotten myself into. And somehow, we made it work. The guests were delighted by the idea of creative American-style sushi. On that night, I decided I wanted to stand in front of customers with confidence and knowledge about sushi.

I searched high and low for a way to gain that knowledge. Just outside of Los Angeles, there was a place that seemed to offer exactly what I was looking for—the California Sushi Academy. Finally, I had the answer. Imagine my surprise when my family and friends asked if I was

Pomegranate and Basil Rolls (page 77)

Making sushi with friends is a great way to catch up while preparing a delicious meal

Mushroom "Spider" Rolls (page 90)

going crazy. Who ever heard of a black female sushi chef?! Couldn't I just be content to continue making sushi in Starkville? I closed the businesses, settled my accounts, and decided to do it anyway.

With every last bit of spunk and chutzpah I had remaining, I boarded a Greyhound bus with a one-way ticket to LA and less than $300 in my pocket. I was practically broke, mostly homeless, and always hungry. But sushi school did not disappoint. It was a magical time of learning and work that I would repeat with no regrets. I soaked up every bit of information available to me. I placed my cutting board as close to the sensei as possible every day. I studied, practiced, and went well beyond my required intern hours before the session was halfway done. And when I finished school, I decided that LA was not the place for a broke, homesick Mississippi girl. I moved to Memphis, Tennessee and began my professional sushi career as the chef of a small local sushi bar.

One of the things I realized while working there was that people wanted to take sushi into their own hands. But it was elusive, and sushi classes often made them feel more intimidated. There were sushi secrets that they wanted to know but couldn't find. I often thought back to

the days when I was trying to learn to make sushi. Why weren't there simple methods? Why couldn't people experiment? And why did sources insist that would-be home chefs buy expensive equipment that they most likely would never use? Necessity had truly been the mother of invention with most of my early sushi recipes and methods. I began a blog and series of workshops to help people create sushi in their home kitchens. And in 2012, *Sushi Secrets: Easy Recipes for the Home Cook* was released.

Why vegetarian sushi?

As soon as I submitted *Sushi Secrets*, I knew that its follow-up had to be a book that focused strictly on vegetarian sushi. One of the biggest things that appealed to me when writing *Vegetarian Sushi Secrets* was that it took a few leaps in the direction of debunking that all-too-familiar myth that sushi must contain raw fish.

What can I say? I suppose I like a challenge...or two. When I shared my intentions, well-meaning family and friends voiced a common concern: "How will you ever come up with enough vegetarian recipes to fill a sushi book?" Yet I found just the opposite problem. Unlike our diminishing access to thinly stretched seafood species, fresh vegetables and fruits are highly accessible. Many

Edamame Hummus (page 45)

Sushi is serious business, as you can see!

communities have a corner specialty grocer or a neighborhood farmers' market. Backyard-gardening enthusiasts are sprouting up everywhere and cultivating that primal urge to dig in and get their hands a little dirty before dinner. With so many options available, it was quite a challenge to look each edible plant family in the eye, so to speak, and deem only some of them sushi-worthy, at least for the purposes of this book.

I am not a vegetarian. Beginning in my teenage years, however, I did spend a little over a decade following a vegetarian lifestyle. During that time I learned many lessons—the biggest being how not to feed a vegetarian. Perhaps my experience with living that lifestyle instilled in me a unique vegetarian sensitivity that I carried over into my world of sushi.

In *Vegetarian Sushi Secrets*, you'll discover potentially problematic ingredients to avoid when stocking your pantry, learn techniques for creating sushi-bar–style sushi, and gain vegetarian-friendly recipes for recreating some of sushi's most famous rolls. You'll encounter some new creations, too, of course. I encourage you to at least read about the different types of sushi before you get ready to roll. Each chapter is organized by sushi techniques, and of-

fers delicious ways to become more familiar with each sushi form. Of course, you can't live on sushi alone, so soups and appetizers, salads and pickles, and desserts and drinks are presented to help create balanced sushi experiences.

In the end, I hope you'll use these methods and recipes as a guide to help you create your own unique style of sushi, or perhaps to learn how to recreate that delicious item from your favorite sushi bar. At the heart of all truly good sushi made in your home kitchen is the knowledge that practice makes perfect, but even mistakes taste incredibly wonderful. If there is any one thing to focus on, it would be to have fun.

Happy Sushi!

*Marisa Baggett*

# Types of Sushi

## Are you ready to roll?

First things first. Having a basic knowledge of sushi types, proper pantry staples, equipment, sushi-rice making, and recipes for sauces and condiments that you will use over and over again is the foundation of sushi success. Learning about various sushi types can expand your horizons. After purchasing sushi pantry staples, prevent waste by learning to store items properly. Improvising and using tools you already have on hand will save money.

When most people think of sushi, maki, or rolled sushi, is what comes to mind. But sushi takes many forms, each with its own unique flavor and preparation.

## NIGIRI SUSHI

Nigiri hand-formed sushi is the crown jewel of sushi. It consists of a bed of rice with a spectacularly simple yet beautiful topping. Even in vegetarian preparations, the most unique and flavorful toppings are draped over a carefully prepared bed of rice. Nigiri is meant to be experienced topping-side first. To eat it, forget the chopsticks! Pick the sushi up with your fingers, flip it upside down, and place it on your tongue topping-side down. If it requires soy sauce, dip the topping rather than the rice to avoid a mess. Many vegetables will require a quick dip in boiling water or a dance across a sauté pan to release their aroma and improve their texture before adorning nigiri sushi.

## INARI SUSHI

Fried tofu that has been simmered in a sweetened soy broth forms an edible pouch for sushi rice. The rice can be stuffed inside the pouch, then covered with assorted toppings. It may also be tossed with other ingredients before being stuffed inside the pouches. Unlike most forms of sushi, inari sushi is not meant to be eaten in a single bite. The filling and the delicious casing that surrounds it are multi-bite delights that deliver a big impact for very little effort.

## GUNKAN-MAKI

Like nigiri sushi, gunkan-maki begins as a little bed of hand-shaped rice. A wide strip of nori is placed around the rice to form a wall that can be filled. The fillings are usually too moist or loose to be used to fill a cut sushi roll. Gunkan-maki are sometimes referred to as "battleship maki," the literal meaning of the name.

## HOSO-MAKI

These are simple, thin sushi rolls that feature the nori on the outside. Inside, a minimal amount of sushi rice is paired with one or perhaps two show-worthy fillings, like a pickle, or a vegetable simmered in flavored broth.

## FUTO-MAKI

If you prefer many fillings at once, these thick sushi rolls will quickly become your favorite. Futo-maki can accommodate an abundance of ingredients. Just keep in mind that thick rolls fall under the one-bite category. No matter how thick, they should be enjoyed in a single bite.

## URA-MAKI

If you've been to a sushi bar, then you will most likely recognize inside-out rolls. As their name implies, the sushi rice is on the outside of the roll. While some may think of this as a way to mask the flavor of the nori, I prefer to think of it as a way to showcase sushi's most vital and most essential element—the sushi rice. Inside-out rolls are extremely versatile, as they can hold multiple fillings. Sometimes, colorful toppings such as avocado are pressed onto the outside of the rolls.

## TEMAKI

For temaki hand rolls, nori is filled with sushi rice and desired fillings, then wrapped into a personal single-serve cone. Hand rolls are not meant to be cut before serving. Enjoy by simply taking bites of the cone.

# Sushi Ingredients

### Avocados

Selecting the right avocados for sushi use is essential. Look for ripe avocados that don't give too much when gently squeezed. Avoid those that are too firm or have bruises. To ripen firm avocados, place them in a closed paper bag near a sunny windowsill.

### Fermented Black Beans

Chinese-style fermented black beans are not usually used in sushi, as they pack a powerful punch that could easily dominate more delicate flavor profiles. Paired with a more robust whole-grain sushi rice, however, a sauce made with these beans is a great topping. Fermented black beans, which contain salt and ginger, can be found in plastic bags at your local Asian market.

### Garlic Chili Paste

Commonly referred to as *sambal oelek*, garlic chili paste is an indispensable condiment for adding spicy flavor to recipes. It is so popular that many supermarkets carry jars of it in the Asian food aisle.

### Panko Japanese Breadcrumbs

*Panko* is another Asian pantry staple that has found popularity in mainstream cooking. Look for plain Japanese-style panko in your grocer's boxed breadcrumb section. Most varieties of panko are vegan.

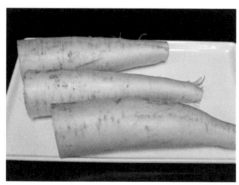

### Daikon Radish

These radishes are long, thick, and root-like in appearance. They can be found in most conventional grocery stores where radishes are sold. Daikon radishes are often cut into sections rather than being sold whole due to their size. Whether buying whole or cut pieces, be sure that they are firm. Exposed areas should not appear spongy. Store daikon in the refrigerator.

### Fresh Ginger Root

When purchasing, look for small, young roots. Avoid ginger roots that are bruised, show signs of mold, or appear dried or overly soggy. Store fresh ginger in your refrigerator for up to two weeks. Chopped or grated ginger may be frozen for up to three months.

### Kampyo

To create this vegetarian sushi filling, strips of Japanese gourd (*calabash*) are shaved into long thin strips and dried. Some large Asian markets will carry the dried strips, but it is most easily found rehydrated and simmered in a sweetened soy and dashi broth liquid. Many conventional supermarket carry pre-simmered kampyo in convenient cans. If adding to sushi rolls, pat away some of the excess liquid. No additional cooking is needed.

## Japanese Cucumbers

Japanese cucumbers are preferred for sushi making because of their thin skins and small, soft seeds. The entire cucumber can be used without overpowering a sushi dish. If using conventional garden cucumbers, peel skins and remove seeds to yield a similar taste.

## Inari Tofu Pouches

*Inari* pouches are made from deep-fried tofu skins (*abura-age*) that are then simmered in a sweetened soy-based liquid. They can be purchased in cans,

plastic-wrapped trays in the refrigerated section, or in frozen packages. Be sure to check the packaging for ingredients. The simmering liquid varies with the manufacturer, and may contain dashi broth made from fish.

## Japanese Soy Sauce

The recipes in this book rely on the flavor profile of Japanese-style soy sauce. A low-sodium variety is suitable for dipping sushi. However, if a recipe uses soy sauce as an ingredient, be sure to use the regular variety. Gluten-free tamari may be used interchangeably with soy sauce in the recipes.

## Kombu

Kombu, a type of kelp, is essential for imparting just the right flavor to dashi stock. It is most commonly found dried and folded into sheets. Look for kombu that is deep green in color. There may be a thin covering of a white powdery substance on the surface. To use, cut away only the amount you need with kitchen shears. Use a damp towel to wipe away the white powdery covering. Kombu should be stored in a cool, dry place.

## Kimchi

This spicy fermented cabbage, borrowed from Korean cuisine, makes an impact in sushi. Kimchi can be purchased in small containers; it is usually refrigerated. Be sure to check the ingredients, as most brands use shrimp paste or dried fish as a flavoring. If unsure of purchased kimchi, see page 49 for a quick do-it-yourself version.

## Matcha Green Tea Powder

Matcha powder can be purchased in small bags or tins. The powder has a very concentrated green color that lends a pleasant tint to recipes. A little goes a long way in imparting the earthy flavor. After opening, store matcha powder in a cool, dark place.

## Mirin

This sweet Japanese cooking wine can be found in most supermarkets where soy sauce is stocked. It is often labeled mirin or *aji-mirin*. If not available, sweet sherry may be substituted.

## Miso Paste

Miso, fermented soybean paste, is available in the refrigerated aisles of Asian markets and health food stores. Miso is most commonly available in white or red paste. A general rule of thumb is that the lighter the color of miso, the more mild and sweet the flavor. The recipes in this book can be made with any variety of miso desired.

## Natto Fermented Soybeans

*Natto* is somewhat of an acquired taste. These fermented soybeans are very pungent, with a slimy texture. When separating natto, the slimy texture is quite visible and looks much like melted cheese strands. Look for natto in the refrigerated section of your local Asian market. Some markets even sell frozen natto in small tubs. Thaw according to package directions and store in the refrigerator.

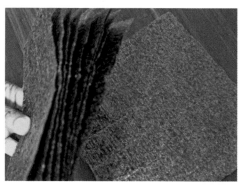

## Nori Seaweed Sheets

Packages of this dried sea vegetable are sold in 8 x 7-inch (20 x 18-cm) sheets. Store nori in a cool, dry place. Seal opened packages in a tight layer of plastic wrap or inside a zip-top plastic bag. When kept dry, nori has an indefinite shelf life.

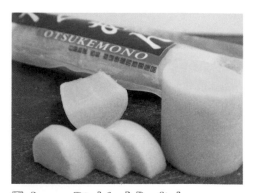

## Takuan Pickled Radish

*Takuan* pickled daikon radish is often bright yellow in color. The pickled daikon portion is usually left whole rather than being pre-cut. Look for *takuan* in plastic pouches in the refrigerated section of your local Asian market.

## Pickled Ginger

This condiment is a sushi favorite. Most familiar is the bright pink dyed variety. It can also be purchased undyed in a natural tan hue. Look for pickled ginger in either non-refrigerated jars or in plastic bags or tubs in the refrigerated section. Store pickled ginger in the refrigerator after opening.

## Quinoa

Though not a grain, quinoa can be cooked like one and used to prepare sushi. Any of the varieties—black, red, or white—can be used. Be sure to use the recipe specifically for quinoa (page 22).

## Rice

Selecting the proper rice for sushi is a top priority, as rice is the foundation of sushi. When purchasing white rice, only medium-grain or short-grain sushi rice must be used. Do not attempt to use jasmine, basmati, white long-grain, or parboiled quick-cooking varieties. Short-grain sushi rice is considered premium, and should be used once you have a few sushi rolling sessions under your belt. Beginners will find that medium-grain sushi rice is easier to handle.

Short-grain brown rice lacks the starch to provide a suitable medium for making rolls. For best results, opt for long-grain brown rice for sushi-making purposes. Do not use rice blends, wild rice, or other whole-grain varieties of rice for sushi. As with white rice, parboiled or quick-cooking varieties of brown rice will not produced the desired results. Be sure to follow the method used only for brown rice when making brown rice sushi (page 23).

## Anko Sweet Red Bean Paste

Sweet *anko* red bean paste is made from red beans and sugar. It is available in cans or in plastic tubs at your local Asian market. After opening, refrigerate any unused portions.

## Rice Vinegar

Rice vinegar is so common that most grocery stores stock it with their other vinegars. Be sure to purchase pure rice vinegar that has not been blended with sugar, salt, or other flavorings. The label should list rice and water as the primary ingredients.

## Sake

For cooking purposes, an inexpensive sake (rice wine) is suitable. If you plan on drinking the sake, too, opt for a midrange brand that is brewed to be served chilled.

## Shichimi Togarashi

The word *shichimi* (or *nanami*) comes from the Japanese word for the number 7. This spicy condiment contains seven different flavors—chili pepper, white sesame seeds, and black sesame seeds, and other seasonings like citrus peel, hemp seed, or ginger. Use it to give your spicy mixtures a unique flavor or as a topping for soups.

## Shiso Leaves

Shiso, or perilla leaf, is an herb that tastes much like a cross between basil and mint. It can be used as a garnish or eaten as-is. Green shiso has a mild pleasant flavor, while the red variety has a robust bite. Shiso can be found at an Asian market; it is also easy to grow at home. (Just be sure to check with your local extension as some areas consider it an invasive weed!) If shiso is unavailable, large sweet basil leaves may be substituted.

## Sorghum Syrup

Unless you have Southern roots, you may be unfamiliar with this sweet syrup. It is cultivated from sweet sorghum grass stalks grown in the southern US. Sorghum syrup, which is vegan, can be used as an equal substitute for honey. Look for it at your local farmer's market or grocery store. Store opened jars in a cool, dark place.

## Sriracha Hot Sauce

The popularity of this spicy pepper sauce makes it easy to find in supermarkets. Store opened bottles in the refrigerator.

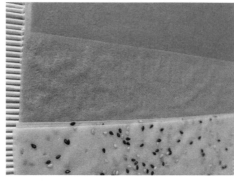

## Soybean Paper

If you have friends who can't stomach the taste and texture of nori, soybean paper could be their saving grace. Unlike nori, soybean paper has a texture and unassuming flavor that most people find agreeable. The sheets can be purchased with or without added flavoring, and they are available in a multitude of colors. Soybean paper can be substituted for nori in any recipe where the sushi rice is on the inside of the roll. Look for soybean paper wrappers in whole or half-sheet sizes. (Use kitchen shears to cut sheets in half.) After opening, store tightly sealed in a cool, dark, dry place.

## Sugar

For best results, use unrefined granulated sugar. If you want to make a sweet substitute, use a granulated natural sweetener. Artificial sweeteners are not recommended.

## Tahini

Tahini, an ingredient that is most commonly found in Mediterranean-style cuisine, is a paste made from pressed, untoasted white sesame seeds. Reminiscent of smooth peanut butter, it usually comes with a thick layer of oil on top. Stir this into the tahini before measuring. Tahini should be stored in the refrigerator after opening.

## Toasted Sesame Oil

When purchasing sesame oil, buy the dark toasted variety. Light sesame oil lacks the depth needed to reproduce the recipes in this book. Like many oils, toasted sesame oil can go rancid. To extend the shelf life, refrigerate opened bottles. The oil will get thick, but quickly becomes fluid again after returning to room temperature.

## Toasted Sesame Seeds

All of the sesame seeds called for throughout this book should be toasted. Black, white, or a mixture of both may be used. To toast, add a thin layer of sesame seeds to a dry skillet over moderately high heat. Swirl the seeds in the skillet, being sure to keep them moving. As they begin to deepen in color and emit a popcorn-like aroma, keep a careful watch. They should be removed from the skillet just before they turn deep brown, as they will continue to toast a few seconds more. Allow to cool completely before use.

## Tofu (firm or extra-firm)

Look for Japanese brands of firm or extra-firm tofu for the recipes in this book. Opt for water-packed varieties in your grocer's refrigerated section. Some varieties can be stored at room temperature until opening. Once opened, be sure

to use the tofu within two or three days. To store opened, unused tofu, place in a container of cool water and refrigerate. Drain and refresh the water each day for optimal freshness.

## Umeboshi Plum Paste

This deep-purple paste has a tangy flavor much like sour candy. It can be purchased in squeeze bottles or small tubs. Treat this condiment like jam or jelly—refrigerate after opening.

## Wakame Seaweed

Wakame is an edible sea vegetable that can be used in soups, salads, and sushi preparations. Look for it in the dried foods section of your local Asian market. To rehydrate, place wakame in warm water and allow to sit for 5 minutes. It will expand quite a bit. Store rehydrated wakame in water in the refrigerator for up to 3 days. For best results, rehydrate in small amounts.

## Wasabi Powder

Look for brands that list wasabi in the ingredients. Store the powder in a tightly sealed container. Wasabi powder is most potent when used just after mixing. Prepare only the amount you'll need for each sushi adventure. To prepare, place 2 or 3 tablespoons of wasabi powder in a small dish. Add 1 teaspoon of water at a time, mixing well with a fork. The consistency should be much like that of toothpaste. Turn the dish upside down on a flat surface until ready to use. Any leftover wasabi paste may be covered and refrigerated. Use within two days.

## Wonton Wrappers

Wonton wrappers come in a variety of styles and shapes. Square wonton wrappers can be easily found in Asian markets and most grocery stores in the refrigerated section.

# Sushi Equipment

It doesn't take a long list of exotic and pricey kitchen tools to prepare great sushi in your home kitchen. In fact, you probably own the most basic tools needed. If you do have to purchase items for your sushi making, they will not sit unused in a dark pantry or kitchen drawer. Most of the tools for a sushi kitchen can be used outside of sushi making.

## Bamboo Rolling Mats

The assembly of most sushi rolls requires the use of a *makisu* or bamboo rolling mat. I find that having two mats is ideal for the sushi-making process. Covering the mats with plastic wrap before each use makes cleanup between different types of sushi rolls much easier. To cover, wrap each mat tightly in two layers of plastic wrap. Hold the mat about 5 inches (13 cm) above the flame of a gas cooktop and move back and forth a few times to tighten the seal. Wash bamboo rolling mats by hand in warm soapy water after use. If overly soiled, gently scrub with a natural bristle brush. Rinse mats well and let stand upright until completely dry.

## Bowls

Maintaining organization during sushi making expedites the process, and having a variety of bowls available is one of the best ways to keep order. Non-reactive plastic, ceramic, or glass bowls in sizes that easily fit into your refrigerator work best, as some ingredients will need to be prepared and stored before use.

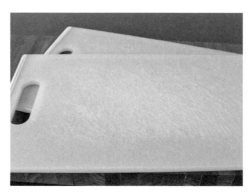

## Cutting Boards

Having several cutting boards simplifies the sushi-making process. I recommend designating cutting boards for specific tasks. A large wooden cutting board with grooves around the edges is perfect for marinating sushi rice. It can be a little messy, but this method is far superior than using a bowl for the task. A large cutting board (plastic or wood) or an inexpensive chopping mat is suitable for both chopping and making sushi rolls.

## Fine-Mesh Colander

A critical step in making sushi rice is allowing time for it to drain. A plastic fine-mesh strainer or colander is best for this task. If using a metal mesh strainer, be careful not to press the rice grains too firmly against it. Washed rice is delicate; individual grains can easily break against the metal, producing rice that is more mushy than toothsome.

## Grater

A fine micro-style grater is preferable to a box grater.

## Knives

Beautiful Japanese sushi knives are nice, but not essential for making sushi at home. A very sharp chef's knife with a blade of at least 10 inches (25 cm) will work just as well.

## Lint-Free Kitchen Towels

Tea towels or flour-sack towels make great towels for sushi. These types of towels are lint free and prevent bits of cloth fibers from finding their way onto your hands and your sushi. For best results, wet towels and keep damp when making sushi.

## Mandoline

To produce thin slices of vegetables in consistent widths, a mandoline is highly recommended.

## Paddles

To marinate the sushi rice, you will need a plastic or wooden paddle. Most rice cookers include a plastic paddle with purchase, and many packs of bamboo rolling mats come with a wooden one. If neither of these is available, use a long-handled wooden spoon. Be sure to soak any wooden utensil in water (or in Sushi Rice Dressing) for at least 10 minutes before using it to toss the sushi rice. Never use a metal utensil to marinate the rice.

## Rice Cooker

For best results, always use a rice cooker to prepare rice for sushi. Not only is it convenient, but it produces the most consistent results. Note the cup capacity on your rice cooker. This refers to the number of cups the rice cooker will accommodate after the rice is cooked. Never add more than two-thirds the amount of rice listed as the rice cooker's full capacity.

## Vegetable Shredder

This special plastic device, made by Benriner, produces excellent garnishes for sushi. You just place a vegetable on the device and turn a crank handle to cut it into thin, curly shreds. It can be purchased online or in Asian markets. Beyond sushi garnishes, it provides an excellent presentation for salad vegetables and makes the coolest shoestring potatoes.

# MAKING PERFECT SUSHI RICE

Sushi rice is the foundation of all great sushi. In fact, a dish can only be considered sushi if it includes sushi rice. Though the unique fillings, toppings, and condiments can enhance the flavor of sushi, it is truly the rice that determines the quality and deliciousness of each sushi dish created.

The careful six-step process of preparing traditional sushi rice using short-grain white rice should yield sufficiently seasoned, toothsome grains that are glossy. Each grain should easily separate from the others while simultaneously remaining sticky. Properly prepared traditional sushi rice should will spread quickly and stick to itself easily. After a bite is taken, the individual grains should disperse evenly across the tongue, giving way for the other ingredients to be experienced.

Heartier grains can be used for making sushi, too. The end result yields a robust flavor and a pleasing texture. Because whole grains lack the stickiness of short-grain white rice, it simply will not do to apply the method used for traditional sushi rice to other grains. The dressing is adjusted to include honey for both flavor and adhesion, while preparation methods also are altered to accommodate the unique properties of each type of grain.

## Sushi Rice Dressing

Nothing about this super-potent dressing should tempt you to eat it on its own. Yet, when added to rice, it produces a delicious and perfectly seasoned rice. Double the recipe and use what's left over as a base for marinated vegetable salads—or save it for your next sushi adventure.

Prep Time: 5 minutes
Makes about 1 cup (250 ml)

¾ cup (185 ml) rice vinegar
⅓ cup (70 g) unrefined sugar, finely ground
3 teaspoons sea salt

Mix together the rice vinegar, unrefined sugar, and sea salt in a small non-metal bowl. Whisk vigorously for about 2 minutes, or until the sugar and sea salt are mostly dissolved. Set aside until ready to use. If making a double batch, store the remainder tightly covered in the refrigerator for up to six weeks. Allow dressing to reach room temperature before use.

# How to Make Traditional Sushi Rice

Don't be put off by the 1½ hours total time needed to complete this version of sushi rice. Most of it is hands-off time. For your patience, you will be rewarded with perfectly flavored rice that spreads easily.

**Prep Time:** 50 minutes
**Cook Time:** 40 minutes
**Makes about 6 cups (1 kg)**

2½ cups (500 g) short-grain white rice
2½ cups (625 ml) water, minus 3 tablespoons
¾ cup (185 ml) Sushi Rice Dressing (page 20)

Place the rice in a medium bowl and cover with cool water. Gently swish the rice in a circular motion with your hand, taking care not to break the grains apart, then pour the water off. Repeat three times.

Place the rice in a fine-mesh strainer and rinse it with cool water. The runoff water should begin to look clear. Allow the rice to drain in the strainer for 10 minutes.

Place the rice and measured water in a rice cooker. Once the rice cooker is started, cook for exactly 40 minutes. Most likely the cooker will indicate that the rice is done before 40 minutes have elapsed, but be patient. Do not lift the lid or stop the process before the time is up.

While the rice cooks, soak a wooden spoon or rice paddle in a shallow bowl of water. This will prevent the cooked rice from sticking to the paddle while tossing with the Sushi Rice Dressing.

Dump the steamed rice onto a large, flat cutting board. With the soaked wooden spoon or paddle, gently "cut" the rice into pieces like a pie. Pour ¼ cup (65 ml) of the Sushi Rice Dressing over the rice and toss well. Continue adding the Sushi Rice Dressing in ¼ cup (65 ml) portions to the rice, tossing well after each addition. Spread the rice into a thin layer and allow to cool for 10 minutes. Gently flip the rice over with the soaked wooden spoon or paddle and let it cool for another 5 minutes.

Place the rice in a large non-metal bowl or container and cover with a damp lint-free dishcloth until ready for use. Use the rice within 4 hours.

Swirl rice with water to wash.

Rinse in a fine-mesh strainer.

Toss hot rice with dressing.

Cover until ready to use.

# Quinoa Sushi "Rice"

Red, white, or black quinoa can be used for this recipe. For a pretty presentation, use a combination of all three. This rice is best used for sushi rolls that feature the seaweed on the outside.

Prep Time: 20 minutes
Cook Time: 40 minutes
Makes about 6½ cups (1⅓ kg)

2½ cups (500 g) quinoa
2½ cups (625 ml) water, minus 3 tablespoons
⅔ cup (160 ml) rice vinegar
⅓ cup (80 ml) raw honey or sorghum syrup
1 tablespoon unrefined sugar
2½ teaspoons coarse sea salt

Multi-Grain Sushi Rice

Place the quinoa in a fine-mesh strainer and rinse it with cool water. Transfer the washed quinoa and measured water to a rice cooker. Once the rice cooker is started, cook for exactly 40 minutes. Most likely the cooker will indicate that the quinoa is done before 40 minutes have elapsed, but be patient. Do not lift the lid or stop the process before the time is up.

While the quinoa cooks, prepare the dressing. Combine the rice vinegar, honey or sorghum, sugar and salt in a small non-metal bowl. Whisk vigorously until the sugar and salt are mostly dissolved, about 2 minutes. Set the mixture aside.

Spoon the steamed quinoa onto a large, flat cutting board. Drizzle ⅓ cup (80 ml) of the dressing over the rice. Toss gently. Add the remaining ⅓ cup (80 ml) of the dressing and toss well.

Spread the quinoa into a thin layer and allow to cool for 10 minutes. Gently turn over and let cool for 5 minutes more.

Place the quinoa in a large non-metal bowl or container and cover with a damp lint-free dishcloth until ready to use. Use within 4 hours.

Quinoa Sushi "Rice"

# Multi-Grain Sushi Rice

Using a variety of grains creates a dense, pleasantly textured medium for sushi. The addition of grits, a Southern breakfast staple, helps to hold all the grains in place. This rice is best used in sushi rolls that feature the seaweed on the outside.

Prep Time: 20 minutes
Cook Time: 40 minutes
Makes about 3 cups (½ kg)

½ cup (100 g) long-grain brown rice
¼ cup (50 g) black, red or white quinoa
¼ cup (50 g) pearled barley
2 tablespoons grits
2 cups (500 ml) water
⅔ cup (160 ml) rice vinegar
⅓ cup (80 ml) raw honey or sorghum syrup
1 tablespoon unrefined sugar
2½ teaspoons coarse sea salt

Toss the brown rice, quinoa, barley and grits into the well of your rice cooker and mix well. Cover with the 2 cups of water. Start the rice cooker and cook for exactly 40 minutes.

Meanwhile, make the dressing. Stir together the rice vinegar, honey or sorghum, sugar, and salt in a small non-metal bowl. Whisk vigorously until most of the sugar and salt have dissolved, about 2 minutes. Set the mixture aside.

When the grains have finished cooking, transfer them to a large glass bowl or casserole dish. Using a plastic or wooden spoon, toss the dressing and grains together. Allow to cool for 10 minutes before using.

# Brown Sushi Rice

The rice may seem overly sticky when it is tossed in the dressing. This is okay. Once it cools to room temperature, the stickiness will be greatly reduced.

Prep Time: 30 minutes
Cook Time: 50 minutes
Makes about 6½ cups (1⅓ kg)

2½ cups (500 g) long grain brown rice
4 cups (1 liter) water
⅔ cup (160 ml) rice vinegar
⅓ cup (80 ml) raw honey or sorghum syrup
1 tablespoon unrefined sugar
2½ teaspoons coarse sea salt

Place the rice in a medium bowl and cover with cool water. Allow to soak for 15 minutes. (Some rice hulls may float to the top. I like to keep them, as the darker flecks give the finished rice character.) Drain the rice in a fine-mesh strainer.

Cook the rice and measured water in a rice cooker for exactly 50 minutes. Do not lift the lid or stop the cooking process before the 50 minutes are up, even if the rice cooker indicates it is done.

Meanwhile, prepare the dressing. Combine the rice vinegar, honey or sorghum, sugar and salt in a small non-metal bowl. Whisk vigorously until most of the sugar and salt have dissolved, about 2 minutes. Set the mixture aside.

Spoon the steamed rice onto a flat cutting board, spreading in a thin layer. It should seem a bit moist and starchy. Drizzle ⅓ cup (80 ml) of the dressing over the rice. Toss gently, then add the remaining ⅓ cup (80 ml) of the dressing and toss well.

Allow to cool uncovered for 10 minutes. Flip the rice over and let cool for 5 minutes. Place in a large non-metal bowl and cover with a damp, lint-free dishcloth until ready to use. Use within 4 hours.

# SAUCES & CONDIMENTS

I am always amazed at the variety of sauces and condiments for sushi that can be created with a handful of the same ingredients. You will already have most of the ingredients stocked in your sushi pantry. While many of these sauce blends and condiments can be purchased, creating them in your own kitchen provides the flexibility to customize them to your tastes as well as to avoid undesired ingredients. Others are unique and will add unexpected flavors to your vegetable sushi creations.

## Amazu Sauce

Heating the vinegar changes the flavor profile and offers a less pungent bite to accompany the sweetness of this sauce.

Prep time: 10 minutes
Cook Time: about 5 minutes
Makes about 2 cups (500 ml)

1 cup (250 ml) rice vinegar
1 cup (250 ml) Vegetarian Dashi (page 27)
3 tablespoons sugar

In a small saucepan, combine the rice vinegar, Vegetarian Dashi and sugar. Heat, stirring constantly, until the sugar dissolves.

Bring mixture to a near boil, then remove from heat. Allow to cool before using. Store leftover sauce in the refrigerator for up to two weeks.

## Miso Dressing

To keep this dressing light in flavor, use a neutral-flavored oil such as avocado, canola or grapeseed oil. For a nuttier flavor, use dark sesame oil or walnut oil.

Prep Time: 15 minutes
Makes about ½ cup (125 ml)

½ cup (125 ml) white miso paste
4 tablespoons Sushi Rice Dressing (page 20)
4 tablespoons water
1 tablespoon soy sauce
1 tablespoon oil

Combine the white miso paste, Sushi Rice Dressing, water and soy sauce in a bowl and mix to combine. Stir in the vegetable oil. Store in the refrigerator for up to one week.

# Sweet Chili Sauce

Bottled versions of this sauce can be found on most grocers' shelves. With just a few ingredients you most likely have on hand, you can create a tastier homemade version.

Prep Time: 5 minutes
Cook Time: 10 minutes
Makes about 1½ cups (375 ml)

1 cup (250 ml) orange juice
½ cup (125 ml) rice vinegar
¼ cup (50 g) sugar
3 teaspoons garlic chili paste, or more, to taste
½ teaspoon finely grated fresh ginger
1 teaspoon potato starch, dissolved in 1 teaspoon water
¼ teaspoon salt

Heat the orange juice, rice vinegar and sugar in a medium saucepan over moderately high heat. Stir until the sugar dissolves and the mixture begins to boil.

Adjust the temperature so that the mixture stays at a low boil. Add the garlic chili paste and the ginger. Stir well.

Whisk in the potato starch mixture and allow to boil for 5 minutes, or until the sauce no longer appears cloudy.

Remove from heat and stir in the salt. The sauce will thicken as it cools.

Serve sauce warm or at room temperature. Refrigerate tightly covered if not using immediately.

# Black Bean Sauce

Black bean sauce isn't traditionally used for sushi, but I find that its robust flavor pairs well with mild vegetables. Fermented black soybeans add a depth of *umami*, a savory basic flavor, to this sauce that cannot be otherwise achieved with substituted ingredients.

Prep Time: 5 minutes
Cook Time: about 5 minutes
Makes about 1 cup (250 ml)

2 teaspoons Chinese black beans
2 tablespoons oil
1 teaspoon finely minced fresh ginger
1 teaspoon finely minced garlic
1 green onion (scallion), thinly sliced
1 cup (250 ml) Vegetarian Dashi (page 27) or
   low-sodium vegetable stock
2 tablespoons rice vinegar
1 tablespoon soy sauce
1 teaspoon salt
1 tablespoon potato starch or cornstarch
   (corn flour), dissolved in 2 tablespoons water

Place the Chinese black beans in a bowl and cover with warm water. Allow to soak for 5 minutes, then drain.

Heat the oil in a skillet over medium heat. Add the ginger, garlic and green onion. Sauté for 1 minute to release fragrances.

Add the Vegetarian Dashi or stock, rice vinegar, soy sauce and salt. Bring the mixture to a boil, then reduce the heat and add the potato starch mixture. Stir well to combine. Cook for 2 minutes, or until sauce begins to thicken.

Refrigerate tightly covered if not using immediately.

# Vegetarian Ponzu Sauce

Store-bought ponzu often contains bonito flakes to enhance the flavor. This vegetarian version relies on a variety of citrus juices to keep the sauce flavor balanced. If you have access to the juice of the yuzu fruit, a uniquely flavored Japanese citrus, use it in place of the lemon juice.

Prep Time: 5 minutes
Resting Time: 24 hours
Makes about 2 cups (500 ml)

1 cup (250 ml) soy sauce
4 tablespoons fresh lemon juice
4 tablespoons fresh white
  grapefruit juice
½ cup (125 ml) fresh lime juice
4 tablespoons rice vinegar
2 tablespoons mirin

Stir all ingredients together in a medium-sized plastic or glass container. (A large glass jar with a lid works just as well.) Be sure to add any fruit pulp to the container. Cover tightly and place in a cool, dark place for 24 hours.

After the mixture has rested, strain it through a fine-mesh strainer. Store Ponzu Sauce in the refrigerator. Bring to room temperature before using.

# Tempura Dipping Sauce

One of the pleasures of Tempura Dipping Sauce is that it is served warm, so be sure to reheat it just before serving. Traditionally, mounds of freshly grated ginger root and freshly grated daikon radish are served alongside this sauce.

Prep Time: 10 minutes
Makes about ¾ cup (185 ml)

½ cup (125 ml) Vegetarian
  Dashi (page 27)
2 tablespoons mirin
2 tablespoons soy sauce

Stir all ingredients together to combine. Refrigerate sauce until ready for use. Heat before serving.

# Vegetarian Eel Sauce

Some brands of eel sauce, a sweetened soy-sauce-based condiment, contain the liquid from cooking sea eels. This vegetarian version is a flavorful substitute. If jaggery or palm sugar are unavailable, use light brown sugar.

Cook Time: 30 minutes (plus time to make Vegetarian Dashi if desired)
Makes about 2¼ cups (565 ml)

1 lb (500 g) brown jaggery or
  palm sugar, roughly chopped
2 cups (500 ml) Vegetarian
  Dashi (page 27) or low-sodium
  vegetable stock
¼ cup (65 ml) sake
¾ cup (185 ml) soy sauce

Combine the jaggery and Vegetarian Dashi or stock in a medium saucepan over medium heat. Stir to dissolve. Add the sake and allow mixture to simmer for about 15 minutes, or until it has reduced by about ¼ cup (65 ml). Stir in the soy sauce and simmer for 10 minutes more. Do not let the mixture boil.

Allow the sauce to cool to room temperature before using. It will thicken as it cools. Store Vegetarian Eel Sauce in the refrigerator.

# Vegetarian Dashi

The leftover mushrooms and kombu kelp can be reused once to make a second batch of dashi. Keep the leftover pieces in a covered container in the refrigerator for up to 3 days. To prepare a second dashi with the leftovers, skip soaking the mushrooms and use fresh water.

**Prep Time:** 5 minutes
**Cook Time:** 5 minutes
**Makes about 2½ cups (625 ml)**

3 cups (750 ml) cool water
2 oz (50 g) dried shiitake mushrooms
One 2 x 2-in (5 x 5-cm) piece kombu kelp

Cover the dried shiitake mushrooms with the water and allow to soak for 5 minutes. Drain the mushrooms, reserving 2½ cups (625 ml) of the soaking water.

Wipe the kombu on both sides with a damp cloth. Bring the reserved shiitake water to a boil in a saucepan. Remove from heat and add the kombu and soaked mushrooms.

Stir all ingredients, and then allow to sit for 5 minutes. Strain away mushrooms and kombu to obtain the dashi liquid.

Soak the mushrooms for 5 minutes.

Wipe the kombu with a damp cloth.

Add kombu and mushrooms to hot water.

Strain the liquid.

# Sesame Dressing

If tahini is unavailable, substitute an equal amount of creamy peanut butter or almond butter. If using homemade Ponzu Sauce, note that it will need to be made a day in advance.

Prep Time: 15 minutes
Makes about ¾ cup (185 ml)

½ cup (125 ml) Ponzu Sauce (page 26)
4 tablespoons sesame paste (tahini)
½ cup (125 ml) water
1 tablespoon dark sesame oil
1 teaspoon grated fresh ginger
½ teaspoon minced garlic
1 green onion (scallion), thinly sliced
1 teaspoon toasted sesame seeds
Pinch of salt, or more, to taste

Combine all ingredients in a small non-metal bowl and stir to combine. Cover and refrigerate for at least 10 minutes before using to allow the flavors to settle. Stir well before using.

# Chia Seed Togarashi

Be sure to use finely chopped dried ginger, not ground ginger powder, in this recipe. To grind the nori, use a clean coffee grinder.

Prep Time: 5 minutes
Makes ½ cup (125 ml)

2 tablespoons black chia seeds
2 tablespoons toasted white sesame seeds
1 teaspoon finely chopped dried orange peel
One 4 x 7-in (10 x 18-cm) nori sheet, finely ground
1 teaspoon cayenne pepper
1 teaspoon red pepper flakes
1 teaspoon hemp seeds
1 teaspoon finely chopped dried ginger root

Place all ingredients in a clean jar. Shake well before using. Store in a cool, dry place.

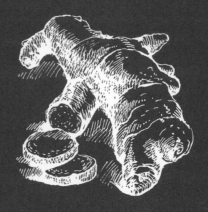

# Ginger Scallion Oil

Try adding a few drops of this oil to soups before serving for extra flavor. This condiment can also be used as the oil in salad dressings.

Prep Time: 10 minutes
Resting Time: 30 minutes
Makes ½ cup (125 ml)

½ cup (125 ml) peanut oil
One ½-in (1.5-cm) length fresh ginger root, peeled and roughly chopped
2 green onions (scallions), thinly sliced
Pinch of salt, or more, to taste

Heat the peanut oil to 350°F (175°C) in a saucepan over high heat. Remove from heat and stir in the fresh ginger root and green onions. Cover with a lid or heavy aluminum foil. Allow to sit for 30 minutes.

Strain the oil. Season with the salt. Leftover oil may be stored in the refrigerator for up to a week.

# Curry Mayonnaise

The flavor of curry pairs well with sweet and tangy sushi rice. Madras curry powder is preferred for the preparation of this mayonnaise.

Prep Time: 5 minutes
Makes about 1 cup (250 ml)

1 cup (250 ml) mayonnaise
1 teaspoon minced garlic
3 teaspoons Madras curry powder
½ teaspoon garlic chili paste
¼ teaspoon cayenne pepper
Pinch of salt, or more, to taste

Combine all ingredients in a small non-metal bowl and mix to combine. Cover and refrigerate for at least 10 minutes before using to allow the flavors to settle.

# Sesame Soy Mustard

This spicy condiment loses its punch after one day, so prepare just enough to use in one sitting.

Prep Time: 5 minutes
Makes 4 tablespoons

4 tablespoons dry mustard powder
3 tablespoons water
2 teaspoons soy sauce
1 teaspoon dark sesame oil

Stir all ingredients together. Let stand for 10 minutes before using to allow the flavors to settle.

# Sorghum Soy Aioli

If you enjoy the flavor of a sweetened soy sauce, this sweet and salty mayonnaise will quickly become a new favorite.

Prep Time: 5 minutes
Makes about 1 cup (250 ml)

1 cup (250 ml) mayonnaise
2 teaspoons minced garlic
3 teaspoons sorghum syrup
2 teaspoons soy sauce
Pinch of salt, or more, to taste

Combine all ingredients in a small non-metal bowl and stir to combine. Cover and refrigerate for at least 10 minutes before using to allow the flavors to settle.

Pumpkin Furikake

# Basic Furikake Seasoning

**Furikake is a seasoning for steamed rice. It also adds variety to seasoned sushi rice. Try any of the variations over sushi rice, on plain tofu or on salads. Furikake also makes a fantastic seasoning for french fries.**

Apple Furikake

**Prep Time: 5 minutes**
**Makes ½ cup (125 g)**

One 4 x 7-in (10 x 18-cm) nori sheet
4 tablespoons toasted sesame seeds
1 teaspoon finely ground golden flax seeds
2 teaspoons salt
½ teaspoon sugar

Use kitchen shears to cut the nori into very thin strips. Place the nori in a food processor and add the sesame seeds, golden flax seeds, sugar and salt. Process until mixed well. Store at room temperature for up to 1 month.

## Variation **Pumpkin Furikake**

Prepare Basic Furikake.

Heat oven to 350°F (175°C). Line a baking sheet with parchment paper. Stir 1 teaspoon of soy sauce into 4 tablespoons of pumpkin purée. Smear thinly across the parchment paper and bake for 15 minutes. Allow to cool, then break into small pieces.

Add pumpkin pieces and 2 tablespoons

Tomato Furikake

chopped roasted pumpkin seeds to the Basic Furikake mix.

## Variation **Apple Furikake**

Prepare Basic Furikake.

Stir in 4 tablespoons finely chopped dried apple chips.

## Variation **Tomato Furikake**

Prepare Basic Furikake.

Heat oven to 350°F (175°C). Line a baking sheet with parchment paper. Stir 1 teaspoon of soy sauce into 4 tablespoons of tomato paste. Smear thinly across the parchment paper and bake for 15 minutes. Allow to cool, then break into small pieces.

Add tomato pieces to the Basic Furikake mix.

## Variation **Curry Furikake**

Prepare Basic Furikake.

Stir in ½ teaspoon celery seeds, ¼ teaspoon cayenne pepper, and 2 teaspoons Madras curry powder.

Curry Furikake

# Chili Daikon

Crisp, peppery daikon is a perfect match for fiery chilies. Try adding a smear or two of Chili Daikon to sushi instead of wasabi paste.

Prep Time: 5 minutes
Makes about ½ cup (125 ml)

One 4-in (10-cm) length daikon radish, peeled
5–8 fresh red chilies

Use a chopstick to poke 5 to 8 holes into the daikon. Insert the chilies into the holes, using the chopstick to help push them in if necessary.

Use a fine grater to grate the daikon into a small bowl. Strain off excess liquid before serving. Leftovers may be stored in the refrigerator for up to 5 days.

Press fresh chilis into daikon radish.

Grate the daikon.

# Chapter 1

# SOUPS & APPETIZERS

For sushi lovers, it may be easy to imagine a meal made entirely of neatly enclosed bites of tangy rice studded with vegetable delights. However, all great sushi experiences begin with something to excite the taste buds. Soups and appetizers should be considered in your overall sushi meal plan to create a more balanced meal. A bowl of soup can warm the belly and open the palate. Tasty morsels of appetizers are often the first glimpse of more good things to come. Practically speaking, a first course also can serve as a way to keep hunger at bay while the sushi is being prepared.

One soup for sipping, served along with one or two appetizers, is generally a good approach to balancing a sushi meal. Let the seasons be your guide if selecting a first course feels daunting. Miso Soup and Soba Noodle Soup are year-round staples that feel appropriate despite the outside temperature. Cold Tofu Trio and Spaghetti Squash Somen are a refreshing cool start to help temper the heat of summer. Warm up the briskness of autumn with a bowl of Clear Soup with Pumpkin Dumplings or Dengaku. Choices for the start of the meal should also balance the sushi in terms of preparation. When preparing sushi with more complex steps, opt for starters that require the simplest preparation methods. If sushi preparation is straightforward, a starter with more involved steps will not feel overly cumbersome.

# Vegetable Tempura

**When making tempura, you must be mindful not only of the temperature of the oil, but also that of the batter and vegetables. Use a deep-fryer thermometer to make sure the oil stays between 335°F (168°C) and 350°F (175°C) to prevent sogginess. Meanwhile, keep the batter cold to produce a lacy and light coating. Vegetables should be at room temperature to minimize the drop in oil temperature when frying.**

**Prep Time:** 15 minutes
**Cook Time:** About 2 minutes per piece
**Makes** 4–6 appetizer servings

**Vegetables**
½ small yellow onion, peeled
2 Japanese eggplants
8 shiitake mushroom caps
8 oz (250 g) asparagus, blanched
8 slices lotus root, peeled and blanched
1 small carrot, peeled and cut into 2-in (5-cm) lengths
½ avocado, cut into 8 wedges
8 shiso (perilla) leaves

**Vegan Tempura Batter**
½ cup (75 g) all-purpose flour
½ cup (75 g) potato starch or cornstarch (corn flour), plus more for dusting
1 cup (125 ml) cold carbonated water
Pinch of salt
Handful of ice cubes

Oil for frying
1 teaspoon grated ginger
1 teaspoon grated daikon radish
Tempura Dipping Sauce (page 26), if desired

Insert toothpicks or short skewers through the onion at ¼ inch (6 mm) intervals. Cut the onion into slices between the toothpicks or skewers. Set aside.

Cut each Japanese eggplant in half lengthwise. Make three long cuts in each half to produce a fan shape. Set aside.

Use a sharp knife to remove a crosshatch section from the top of each shiitake mushroom cap. Set aside.

Have all other vegetables ready. Heat at least 2 inches of oil in a skillet or wok to 350°F (175°C).

Make the tempura batter: In a small bowl, stir together the flour, potato starch, carbonated water, and salt. Add the ice cubes. The batter will be thin.

Dredge three or four vegetable pieces in potato starch and shake off the excess.

Dip the vegetable pieces into the cold batter. You should still be able to see the vegetables through the batter.

Gently slide the dipped vegetables into the hot oil. Be careful not to drop ice into the hot grease. Fry until crisp, about 2 minutes. The eggplants will need to be flipped over and fried for about 2 minutes more.

Use a slotted spoon to remove vegetables from oil. Allow to drain on a wire rack. Discard the beads of batter that float in between batches.

Repeat with remaining vegetable pieces, a few at a time, monitoring the heat of the oil.

Arrange cooked Vegetable Tempura on a platter. Serve with warm Tempura Dipping Sauce, if desired, with grated daikon radish and ginger on the side.

Heat the oil to 350°F (175°C).

Stir together the batter ingredients.

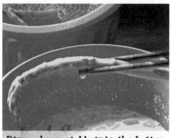
Dip each vegetable into the batter.

Fry the vegetables until crisp.

Drain vegetables on a wire rack.

# Soba Noodle Soup

Adding tempura to soup feels very much like adding crackers to soup. The hard crackers soften a bit in the warm broth, while still remaining a little crunchy. Any sort of tempura vegetable, like mushrooms, blanched asparagus, and onions, will compliment this soup. My favorite is tempura avocado. Whatever vegetable you select, be sure to add it to the soup immediately before serving so it doesn't get soggy.

**Prep Time: 15 minutes**
**Cook Time: About 15 minutes**
**Makes 4 servings**

4 cups (1 liter) Vegetarian Dashi (page 27) or low-sodium vegetable stock
1 tablespoon soy sauce
1 tablespoon mirin
½ tablespoon sake
6 oz (175 g) dried soba noodles
2 inari pouches, cut into thin strips
8 pieces prepared Vegetable Tempura (see recipe on opposite page)
One 4 x 7-in (10 x 13-cm) nori sheet, cut into thin strips
2 green onions, thinly sliced

In a medium saucepan, bring the Vegetarian Dashi to a low simmer. Add the soy sauce, mirin and sake. Allow to simmer for 5 minutes.

Bring 4 quarts (3.75 liters) unsalted water to a boil. Add the soba noodles and cook for about 7 minutes, or until the soba is cooked through, but still firm. Drain in a colander and rinse well with warm water.

Divide the noodles evenly among 4 bowls. Spoon 1 cup (250 ml) of hot broth over each bowl of noodles.

Distribute the Vegetable Tempura pieces, inari pouch strips, nori strips, and green onions equally among the four bowls. Serve immediately.

# Clear Soup with Pumpkin Dumplings

A little bit of toasted pumpkin seed oil goes a long way. Its earthy, robust flavor is very similar to that of toasted sesame oil. If you don't have toasted pumpkin seed oil, use an equal amount of dark sesame oil instead.

Prep Time: 30 minutes
Cook Time: 3 minutes
Makes 6 servings

**Dumplings**
1 cup (220 g) pumpkin puree
1 square Japanese curry base
3 green onions (scallions), thinly sliced
2 teaspoons minced garlic
½ bunch fresh coriander leaves (cilantro), roughly chopped
4 teaspoons soy sauce
½ cup (30 g) panko breadcrumbs

18 square wonton wrappers
2 teaspoons potato starch, dissolved in 4 teaspoons water

**Clear Soup**
3 teaspoons toasted pumpkin seed oil
3 teaspoons roasted pumpkin seeds
12 oz (350 g) extra-firm tofu, cut into ½-in (1.25-cm) cubes
6 cups (1.5 liters) Vegetarian Dashi (page 27), heated
3 green onions (scallions), thinly sliced, if desired

Place a large pot of water over high heat. Bring to a boil.

To prepare the dumplings, combine the pumpkin puree, Japanese curry base, green onions, garlic, coriander leaves, soy sauce and panko breadcrumbs in a food processor. Pulse a few times, then process until well blended.

Place two wonton wrappers on your work surface. (Keep the remaining wrappers covered with a damp towel.) Spoon 1 tablespoon of the pumpkin mixture in the center of each wrapper. Dip a fingertip in the potato starch mixture and wet the edges of the wonton wrapper. Pull the edges of the wrapper around the mixture and pinch closed. Fold the dumpling so the ends meet and crimp to close. Repeat with the remaining wrappers and filling.

Gently drop the dumplings in the boiling water and then turn off the heat. Stir with a spoon to make sure none of the dumplings stick to the bottom of the pot. Let dumplings cook for 3 minutes. Remove from the pot with a slotted spoon.

To assemble the soup, lay out 6 medium-sized soup bowls. Place ½ teaspoon pumpkin seed oil and ½ teaspoon pumpkin seeds in each bowl. Divide the tofu evenly among the bowls. Add 3 warm dumplings to each bowl. Ladle 1 cup (250 ml) of hot dashi into each bowl. Sprinkle with green onions, if desired. Serve immediately.

# Cold Tofu Trio

For many years, I was squeamish about tofu. Grilled, fried and sautéed versions that promised to taste "just like" their meat or fish counterparts left nothing but a bad taste in my mouth. It wasn't until I was urged to try tofu as tofu—cold, unpretentious bites of creamy goodness—that I began to appreciate it.

Be sure to use the absolute best quality extra-firm tofu you can find for this trio. Chill the tofu before preparing the dish, or serve at room temperature.

Prep Time: 10 minutes
Makes 6 servings

Two 12-oz (350-g) blocks firm tofu
4 tablespoons Amazu Sauce (page 24)
1 tablespoon grated ginger
1 tablespoon grated daikon radish
2 tablespoons shredded carrot
4 tablespoons Vegetarian Eel Sauce (page 26)
2 tablespoons fried onions (I like to use French's)
8 cherry tomatoes, halved
4 tablespoons Vegetarian Ponzu Sauce (page 26)
1 green onion (scallion), finely sliced

Have ready 3 small serving dishes with shallow sides.

Cut each block of tofu into 6 even squares. Arrange four squares of tofu on each serving dish.

On the first dish, spoon the Amazu Sauce over the tofu. Add the ginger in a mound on top, followed by the daikon. Arrange the shredded carrots around the tofu.

On the second dish, spoon the Vegetarian Eel Sauce over the tofu. Sprinkle the fried onions on top.

For the third dish, arrange the cherry tomatoes over the tofu. Spoon the Vegetarian Ponzu Sauce over the tomatoes and tofu. Sprinkle with green onions.

Serve immediately.

# Wasabi Deviled Eggs

**For faster preparation, use a package of pre-boiled, pre-peeled eggs.**

**Prep Time:** 10 minutes
**Cook Time:** 20 minutes
**Makes 1 dozen**

6 eggs
1 teaspoon wasabi powder
2 teaspoons water
½ teaspoon prepared horseradish
½ teaspoon mustard
4 tablespoons mayonnaise
1 teaspoon soy sauce
Pinch of salt
Basic Furikake Seasoning (page 30),
    to taste

Place eggs in a medium-sized saucepan and cover with cold water. Bring to a boil over high heat. Remove pan from heat and cover tightly. Let sit undisturbed for 18 minutes.

While the eggs cook, prepare the wasabi mayonnaise. Stir together the wasabi powder and the water. Add the prepared horseradish, mustard, mayonnaise and soy sauce. Stir well.

Rinse eggs with cool water before peeling. Cut eggs in half lengthwise and scoop out yolks.

Place yolks in a bowl. Add the wasabi mayonnaise and salt. Mash and stir with a fork until the mixture is smooth.

Divide the egg yolk mixture evenly between the boiled egg halves.

Chill for at least 30 minutes. Sprinkle generously with Basic Furikake Seasoning just before serving.

## Variation
### Sriracha Deviled Eggs

Prepare the boiled eggs as described at left. Omit the wasabi powder, water, horseradish and mustard. Stir 1 tablespoon of sriracha sauce into the mayonnaise. Place the yolks in a bowl and add the sriracha mayonnaise, soy sauce and salt. Divide the egg yolk mixture evenly between the eggs and chill for at least 30 minutes. Garnish each egg with additional sriracha sauce, to taste.

# Eggplant Dengaku (Broiled Miso Eggplant)

**Soaking the eggplant in heavily salted water works wonders. The salt draws out the bitterness and leaves behind a pleasant, fresh taste. The overall texture of the cooked eggplant will be simultaneously firm and creamy. Use this technique before preparing any eggplant dish and everyone will wonder why your eggplant is always so tasty!**

Prep Time: 15 minutes
Cook Time: 8 minutes
Makes 4 servings

4 Japanese eggplants or 2 medium-sized globe
   eggplants
4 tablespoons salt
1 cup (275 g) miso
4 teaspoons sugar
4 teaspoons mirin
2 tablespoons sesame oil
Toasted sesame seeds, to taste

Cut each eggplant in half lengthwise. Fill a large bowl or pot with lukewarm water and mix in the salt. Place the eggplant halves in the bowl, weight down with a lid or plate, and let stand for 10 minutes.

In a small saucepan, combine the miso, sugar and mirin over medium heat. Stir constantly until mixture comes to a near boil. Set aside.

Preheat oven to 400°F (200°C). Remove the eggplant halves from the salt water and pat dry. Cut a few shallow slits into each half. Rub with sesame oil and place face down on a baking sheet. Roast for 5 minutes, or until the eggplants feel soft in the center.

Remove the eggplants from the oven. Turn broiler to high. Flip the eggplants over so that the cut side is facing upwards. Brush each eggplant with a generous amount of the miso mixture. Sprinkle the toasted sesame seeds over. Broil the eggplants for 3 minutes or until the topping is caramelized. Serve immediately.

# Vegetable Gyoza

If this recipe yields more dumplings than you can eat in one sitting, cook them all and then store the extra ones in the freezer. Fully cooked dumplings freeze well and can be microwaved straight from the freezer for an anytime snack. To cook frozen dumplings, place the desired amount on a microwave-safe plate. Cover with a paper towel and cook on high for about 45 seconds to 1 minute.

**Prep Time:** 20 minutes
**Cook Time:** 5 minutes per batch
**Makes about 30 gyoza**

**Gyoza Dipping Sauce:**
¾ cup (185 ml) soy sauce
4 tablespoons rice vinegar
1 teaspoon dark sesame oil
1 teaspoon sesame seeds
2 green onions (scallions) sliced
1 teaspoon red pepper flakes

**Gyoza Filling:**
4 tablespoons oil (more if needed)
½ lb (250 g) shiitake mushrooms
½ lb (250 g) spinach
½ lb (250 g) cabbage, finely chopped
2 teaspoons minced garlic
2 teaspoons grated fresh ginger
2 green onions (scallions), sliced
3 tablespoons soy sauce
1 teaspoon salt
2 teaspoons dark sesame oil
About 30 gyoza wrappers
1 tablespoon potato starch or cornstarch (corn flour), dissolved in 2 tablespoons water

Prepare the Gyoza Dipping Sauce: Stir together the soy sauce, rice vinegar, sesame oil, sesame seeds, green onions and red pepper flakes. Set aside at room temperature.

Heat 2 tablespoons of the cooking oil in a skillet over medium heat. Sauté the shiitake mushrooms and spinach until mushrooms are soft, about 5 minutes.

Allow to cool.

Place the shiitake mushroom and spinach mixture, cabbage, garlic, fresh ginger, green onions, soy sauce, salt and dark sesame oil in a food processor. Pulse several times and then process into a thick paste-like mixture.

Working with 6 gyoza wrappers at a time, place 1 teaspoon of the mushroom

mixture in the center of each wrapper. Dip a finger in the potato starch mix and wet the outer rims of the wrappers.

Fold the edges over to form half-moon shapes and press tightly to seal. Set aside and cover with a damp towel. Repeat in batches of 6 with the remaining mixture.

Heat just enough of the remaining oil to coat the bottom of the bottom of a skillet with a fitted lid. Place 5 or 6 dumplings in the pan and allow to sear until the bottom becomes brown and crisp, about 1½ minutes. Using the lid to shield yourself from oil spattering, pour ¼ cup (65 ml) water into the skillet. Cover quickly. Cook the dumplings at least 3 minutes or until the water is almost gone.

Remove the dumplings from the skillet with a spatula. Rinse and dry the skillet and repeat the steps for cooking with the remaining dumplings.

Serve warm with Gyoza Dipping Sauce.

## Variation
### Kimchi Gyoza

Omit the shiitake mushrooms, spinach, cabbage, garlic and ginger. Drain 1 lb (500 g) of kimchi. Place in a food processor with 4 tablespoons tomato paste. Add the green onions, soy sauce, salt and dark sesame oil. Pulse several times, then process for 30 seconds. Follow the method given above for assembling then cooking the dumplings. Serve warm with Gyoza Dipping Sauce.

Make the dipping sauce.

Sauté the spinach and mushrooms until soft.

Process ingredients into a thick paste.

Work with no more than 6 wrappers at a time.

Place 1 tablespoon of filling in center of wrapper.

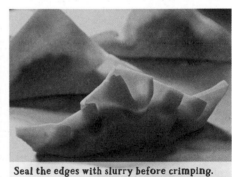
Seal the edges with slurry before crimping.

Sear dumplings until lightly browned.

Add ¼ cup (65 ml) water to skillet and cover.

# Tempura Brie with Three Sauces and Ginger Snaps

Years ago, at a bed and breakfast where I worked, the chef set out a small bowl of thin gingersnap cookies next to the Brie on every cheese platter. After one taste of the combo, I was hooked. Thin crumbly Swedish ginger snaps pair better than the thicker, hard ones.

**Prep Time: 45 minutes**
**Cook Time: 5 minutes**
**Makes 3 servings**

½ cup Vegetarian Eel Sauce
    (page 26)
½ cup (125 ml) Sweet Chili
    Sauce (page 25)
½ cup (125 ml) Amazu Sauce
    (page 24)
1 teaspoon fresh orange zest
4 oz (115 g) cherries, pitted
    and cut in half

1 cup (150 g) flour
1 cup (250 ml) soda water
1 egg
Peanut oil for frying
½ cup (75 g) potato starch or
    cornstarch (corn flour)
One 8 oz (230 g) wedge Brie,
    frozen at least 45 minutes
Thin ginger snaps (optional)

Stir the orange zest into the Sweet Chili Sauce. Toss the cherries with the Amazu Sauce. Set sauces aside.

In a medium bowl, stir together the flour, soda water and egg. The mixture will be lumpy.

Heat at least 2 in (5 cm) of the oil to 350°F (175°C) in a skillet or wok.

Dredge the frozen Brie in potato starch, then dip in the tempura batter. Dip again in the potato starch and then the tempura batter. Gently lower the Brie into the hot oil. Use a chopstick or cooking spoon to make sure it doesn't stick to the bottom of the skillet or wok.

With a spoon, drizzle some of the tempura batter over the Brie as it cooks. Fry for 2 minutes or until golden brown.

Remove from the oil and drain on a wire rack.

Place fried Brie on a serving platter. Serve immediately with sauces and ginger snaps, if desired.

# Spaghetti Squash Somen

Traditional somen noodles are delicate wheat flour noodles that are often served in a bowl of ice water with a side of dipping sauce. Spaghetti squash offers a fun take on tradition. This dish is great for lunch on a hot summer day or on an especially warm autumn afternoon.

**Prep Time:** 30 minutes
**Cook Time:** about 35 minutes
**Makes 4 servings**

1 medium spaghetti squash
½ cup (125 ml) Vegetarian Dashi (page 27) or water

**Dipping Sauce:**
2 tablespoons mirin
2 tablespoons sake
4 tablespoons soy sauce
1 teaspoon sugar
1 cup (250 ml) Vegetarian Dashi (page 27)

2 teaspoons toasted sesame seeds
4 green onions (scallions), finely chopped
2 teaspoons grated fresh ginger

Preheat oven to 400°F (200°C).

Cut the spaghetti squash in half lengthwise. Scoop out and discard the seeds and pulp. Place cut side down on a roasting pan. Pour the ½ cup Vegetarian Dashi or water into pan and cover with aluminum foil. Roast for 30 minutes, or until a fork easily pierces the flesh.

While the squash is roasting, prepare the sauce. In a small saucepan, heat the mirin and sake over medium high heat for 2 minutes to cook off alcohol. Add the soy sauce, sugar and 1 cup Vegetarian Dashi. Cook for 2 minutes more, stirring often. Remove from heat and allow to cool to room temperature. Refrigerate at least 10 minutes before using.

When the squash is ready, drag a fork across the flesh side to create thin strands. Remove the "noodles" from the skin and allow to cool before refrigerating. Refrigerate at least 30 minutes.

Divide squash among 4 serving dishes. Sprinkle evenly with sesame seeds. Provide dipping sauce for each person, as well as a dish with green onions and fresh ginger root. To eat, dip the "noodles" in the green onions and fresh ginger before dipping in the sauce.

## Variation
### Ponzu Garlic Somen
Toss chilled "noodles" with 2 tablespoons olive oil, 1 teaspoon grated garlic and 4 oz (120 g) halved cherry tomatoes. Provide Furikake Seasoning (page 30) and Vegetarian Ponzu Sauce (page 26) for dipping.

# Tofu Miso Soup

The lightly flavored broth is enhanced by salty miso. Creamy cubes of tofu float in the bowl as the flavor of the sea makes its way across your taste buds thanks to the flavorful wakame.

Prep Time: 5 minutes
Cook Time: 5 minutes
Makes 4 servings

2 teaspoons dried wakame seaweed
4 cups (1 liter) Vegetarian Dashi (page 27)
1 cup (275 g) miso
12 oz (350 g) tofu, cut into ½-in (1.25-cm) cubes (use more if desired)

Place the dried wakame in small bowl filled with lukewarm water. Allow to reconstitute for at least five minutes. Pour off excess water.

Bring the dashi to a simmer in a pot over medium heat, but do not allow it to boil. Add the miso to the pot and whisk until smooth.

Remove the dashi mixture from the heat and set aside.

Prepare 4 bowls for soup. Divide the reconstituted wakame and tofu among the four bowls. Ladle 1 cup (250 ml) of the dashi mixture into each bowl. Serve immediately.

# Soy Glazed Sweet Potatoes

These are addictive. Try dipping them in Sorghum Soy Aioli (page 29). For a side dish, brush the sweet potatoes with butter instead of oil before roasting.

Prep Time: 10 minutes
Cook Time: 25 minutes
Makes 8 servings

4 large sweet potatoes (preferably unpeeled), cut into wedges
Oil for roasting
½ cup (125 ml) molasses or sorghum syrup
4 tablespoons water
4 tablespoons soy sauce

Preheat the oven to 400°F (200°C). Brush the sweet potato wedges generously with oil. Arrange the wedges on a heavy-bottomed baking sheet so that they do not touch. Roast for 15 minutes.

While the sweet potatoes roast, prepare the glaze. Bring the molasses and water to a boil in a medium saucepan. Cook for 5 minutes. Remove the mixture from the heat and stir in the soy sauce.

After the potatoes have roasted for 15 minutes, carefully pour the molasses mixture over them. Toss gently with tongs. Roast the potatoes for 5 more minutes or until tender.

Serve hot or at room temperature.

# Edamame Hummus

A nice bowl of this delicious hummus is a crowd pleaser—as long as the crowd knows it's not a bowl of wasabi! Set aside a few of the whole cooked edamame beans for a garnish. Placing those on top of the finished dish along with a splash of sesame oil helps to make the distinction.

Prep Time: 10 minutes
Cook Time: 5 minutes
Makes about 2 cups (500 ml)

One 16 oz (500 g) package shelled edamame
    (green soybeans)
½ cup (125 ml) water
Juice of 1 lemon
2 teaspoons soy sauce
1 teaspoon tahini
1 teaspoon dark sesame oil
½ teaspoon minced garlic
¼ teaspoon ground coriander
1 teaspoon salt, or more, to taste

Boil or steam the edamame according to package instructions. Drain and cool to room temperature.

Place the cooled edamame, water, lemon juice, soy sauce, tahini, sesame oil, garlic, ground coriander and salt in a high-powered blender or food processor. Pulse a few times before blending or processing. (If it seems to be moving slowly, stop the appliance immediately. Add about 4 tablespoons of water and pulse again before blending or processing to keep the motor from burning out.)

Continue blending or processing until the hummus is smooth and creamy.

Store covered in the refrigerator for up to 4 days.

# Chapter 2

# SALADS & PICKLES

Tangy sushi rice is a fine companion for salads and pickles featuring pungent, sharp flavors. Salads can be prepared quickly. Select a salad as a fresh first course, or use it in smaller quantities as a delicious addition to sushi platters. Pairing a sushi roll with a hearty serving of salad makes for a fulfilling lunch or casual dinner.

Pickles require more patience than salads, but the end result completely justifies the wait. Preparation is often simple and fast, but pickles can take anywhere from several minutes to several days to mature. Select a few pickles to keep on hand or use for an upcoming sushi experience. They keep well for weeks in the refrigerator when stored in plastic, glass or ceramic containers.

Party Spinach Salad and Quick Cucumber Salad are low-key crowd pleasers, while Miso Asparagus Salad and Crispy Eggplant with Fragrant Wilted Greens Salad are more suitable for enjoying in small gatherings. Pickled Ginger is a sushi staple that deserves to be made at least once at home. You may never return to the store-bought variety. Pickled Lotus Root and its spicy alternative are a little more exotic. Try them when you're feeling a bit more adventurous.

# Crispy Eggplant with Fragrant Wilted Greens Salad

**Serve this dish at room temperature, rather than piping hot. You'll find the flavors more pronounced. Add a handful of your favorite chopped nuts to make a complete meal.**

**Prep Time: 15 minutes**
**Cook Time: 10 minutes**
**Makes 4 Servings**

2 medium-sized eggplants
Generous pinch of salt, plus more
   for soaking eggplant
1 cup (150 g) potato starch
1 teaspoon onion powder
1 teaspoon garlic powder

Oil for frying
1 lb (500 g) arugula
1 cup (250 ml) Sweet Chili Sauce
   (page 25), warmed
1 bunch green onions (scallions),
   chopped
1 bunch fresh coriander leaves
   (cilantro), chopped
1 bunch mint, chopped

Cut the eggplants into ½-inch (1-cm) cubes and place in a large non-metal bowl. Cover with water, add salt and stir. Cover (or weigh down with a plate) and allow to stand for 10 minutes. (This draws the bitterness out of the eggplant.)

Drain the eggplant cubes and place on paper towels to dry. In a large bowl, stir together the potato starch, onion powder, garlic powder and an additional pinch of salt. Toss the eggplant with the potato starch mixture, covering as much surface area as possible. Shake off any excess.

In a large frying pan over medium heat, add oil to a depth of about ½ inch (1.25 cm). Heat to 350°F (175°C). Add the eggplant cubes and fry until golden brown on all sides, about 2 minutes. Drain on paper towels.

In a skillet, heat an additional 2 tablespoons of oil over high heat. Add the arugula and sauté until the greens just begin to wilt, about 1 minute. Arrange the wilted arugula around the edge of a serving platter and top with the fried eggplant. Pour warmed Sweet Chili Sauce on top. Garnish with chopped green onions, coriander leaves, and mint. Serve immediately.

# Vegan Kimchi

Kimchi is another one of those tasty dishes that often contains dried seafood. If that isn't your thing, here's a version you can make at home. The best part? It's relatively instant gratification: it can be ready in less than an hour.

**Prep Time:** 45 minutes
**Makes about 1½ lbs (750 grams)**

1 small napa cabbage, cut into large chunks
1 carrot, peeled and shredded
1 small yellow onion, thinly sliced
One 1-in (2.5-cm) length daikon radish, peeled and thinly sliced
4 green onions (scallions), thinly sliced
3 oz (85 g) pea sprouts
½ cup (135 g) salt, plus a generous pinch
1 tablespoon turbinado sugar
1 tablespoon miso paste
1 tablespoon grated fresh ginger
½ cup (125 ml) garlic chili paste
2 tablespoons rice vinegar
1 teaspoon cayenne pepper

Place the napa cabbage, carrot, onion, daikon, green onions and pea sprouts in a medium bowl. Cover with the two tablespoons of salt and toss several times. The vegetables should begin to release a small amount of water. Allow to sit for 10 minutes, then rinse thoroughly and drain. Squeeze the vegetables to release excess water.

Combine the turbinado sugar, miso paste, fresh ginger, garlic chili paste, rice vinegar, cayenne pepper and pinch of salt, and stir to combine. Add to the vegetables and stir well to coat each piece.

Allow the kimchi to sit at room temperature for at least 30 minutes before using. Store leftovers in refrigerator for up to 1 week.

# Quick Cucumber Salad

If you like your cucumbers with a little kick, add a teaspoon of garlic chili paste to the bowl before tossing together the ingredients.

Prep Time: 5 minutes
Marinating Time: 10 minutes
Makes 4 servings

6 Japanese cucumbers or 2 English cucumbers, thinly sliced
¾ cup (185 ml) Sushi Rice Dressing (page 20)
1 teaspoon sesame oil
1 teaspoon toasted sesame seeds

Combine all ingredients in a small non-metal mixing bowl and toss together. Allow flavors to develop for 10 minutes at room temperature. Serve at room temperature or refrigerate for up to 2 days. To serve, pour off any excess liquid and then divide the salad among 4 small bowls.

# Miso-Pickled Eggplant

You can reuse this pickling medium several times. Simply add more salted eggplant and stir thoroughly. You'll know it's time to start fresh when the miso begins to get thin and watery.

Prep Time: 15 minutes
Pickling Time: 4 hours or up to 2 days
Makes about 6 servings

1 cup (275 g) miso
2 teaspoons mirin
1 teaspoon finely grated fresh ginger
1 teaspoon minced garlic
2 small Japanese eggplants or 1 globe eggplant, cut into ¼ in (5 mm) rounds or half-moons
2 tablespoons salt

In a glass container, combine the miso, mirin, grated ginger and garlic. Stir well and then set aside.

Place eggplant in a bowl filled with water. Add the salt. Weight the eggplant with a plate or heavy lid and allow to sit for 10 minutes.

Drain the eggplant. Rinse thoroughly and pat dry.

Add the eggplant to the miso mixture and stir to coat each piece thoroughly with miso. Cover and allow to sit at room temperature for 4 hours.

For a light pickle, remove eggplant from miso. Rinse off excess miso before enjoying. For a more flavorful pickle, refrigerate the covered dish and allow to sit undisturbed for 2 days before removing eggplant. Be sure to rinse off excess miso before serving.

Cut ginger into paper-thin slices.

Salt the ginger.

# Pickled Ginger

**If you don't have a mandoline, use a vegetable peeler to slice the ginger root as thinly as possible.**

**Prep Time: 25 minutes**
**Makes about 4 servings**

One 2-in (5-cm) length fresh ginger
  root, peeled and thinly sliced
4 tablespoons salt
1 cup (250 ml) Sushi Rice Dressing
  (page 20)
3 tablespoons mirin (sweet rice wine)
  or sweet sherry

Place the ginger slices in a colander and cover with salt. Allow to sit for 10 minutes, then rinse away the salt.

In a clean glass or ceramic container, combine the Sushi Rice Dressing and mirin or sweet sherry. Add the sliced ginger and toss to coat.

Allow to sit for at least 10 minutes before using. Store leftovers in the refrigerator for up to one month.

## Variation
**Pink Ginger**
Add a slice of fresh beetroot to the glass container with the ginger and dressing. Stir or shake well for 2 minutes. Discard the beet slice before using the ginger.

Toss ginger with dressing and mirin.

For pink ginger, add beet and stir or shake.

# Miso Asparagus Salad

**Since the asparagus is raw, you'll want to use the freshest spears possible. Avoid asparagus with overly thick stalks, as these tend to be tough. For best results, make this salad when asparagus is in season.**

**Prep Time:** 15 minutes
**Makes 4–6 servings**

1 lb (500 g) fresh asparagus
½ cup (125 ml) Miso Dressing (page 24)
Shaved Parmesan cheese, to taste
  (optional)

Wash the asparagus and trim off the rough ends.

Fill a medium-sized bowl with cold water and add some ice cubes. Use a vegetable peeler to shave the asparagus spears. Place the shavings in the cold water until they begin to get curly.

Drain the shaved asparagus. Place in a large bowl and toss with Miso Dressing.

Serve immediately with shaved Parmesan cheese, if desired.

# Pickled Lotus Root

It is not uncommon to slice open a lotus root and find that it is dirty inside. To clean, place lotus root slices in a bowl of cool water. Swish them around for a few seconds, then allow them to sit undisturbed. The lotus root slices will float to the top and the dirt will settle at the bottom of the bowl.

Prep Time: 10 minutes
Cook Time: 1½ minutes
Makes 4 servings

One 2-in (5-cm) length of fresh lotus root,
   peeled and thinly sliced
1 cup (250 ml) Sushi Rice Dressing (page 20)
1 teaspoon grated beetroot

Peel the lotus root and cut into very thin slices.

Bring approximately 4 cups (1 liter) of water to a boil. Add the lotus root slices and blanch for 90 seconds, then plunge in ice water to cool completely.

Drain the lotus root slices, pat dry, and place in a ceramic or glass container. Add the Sushi Rice Dressing and grated beetroot. Toss well. Allow to stand at room temperature for 10 minutes for flavors to develop.

Serve Pickled Lotus Root at room temperature or chilled. Refrigerate leftovers for up to 5 days.

## Variation
### Spicy Pickled Lotus Root
Omit the fresh beetroot. Toss the blanched lotus root and the Sushi Rice Dressing with 1 sliced serrano pepper, ½ teaspoon grated fresh ginger root, 1 smashed garlic clove and 1 thinly sliced green onion (scallion). Allow the mixture to stand at room temperature for 10 minutes before serving.

# Kale with Sesame Dressing

**Use your favorite variety of kale for this salad. Even chopped collards or mustard greens can be substituted. The key to the salad is massaging the greens with the dressing. This helps to break down the coarse veins in the leaves and takes away the bitter "raw" flavor.**

**Prep Time: about 10 minutes**
**Makes 4 servings**

1 lb (500 g) kale, trimmed and chopped into
  bite-sized pieces
½ cup (125 ml) Sesame Dressing (page 28)
1 teaspoon toasted sesame seeds
4 tablespoons dried cherries
2 green onions (scallions), thinly sliced
½ cup (40 g) toasted slivered almonds

Place the kale in a large mixing bowl and add the Sesame Dressing. Gently massage the kale and dressing together for 2 minutes.

Add the sesame seeds, dried cherries, green onions and slivered almonds. Toss well.

Serve immediately or refrigerate for up to 2 days.

# Daikon Slaw

If you need a make-ahead side dish, look no further. Daikon holds up well when refrigerated; this slaw tastes fresh even after 4 or 5 days.

Prep Time: 5 minutes
Marinating Time: 1 hour
Makes 2 servings

One 4-in (10-cm) length daikon radish, peeled
2 large carrots
2 teaspoons finely grated fresh ginger
4 tablespoons Sushi Rice Dressing (page 20)

Shred the daikon radish and carrot. Toss together with the grated ginger. Add the Sushi Rice Dressing and stir well.

Chill for at least 1 hour before serving. Serve cold.

## Variation
### Pomegranate Slaw
Add ⅓ cup (85 g) pomegranate seeds (arils) and ½ teaspoon finely chopped fresh jalapeño pepper to the shredded daikon and carrot. Toss with the fresh ginger and Sushi Rice Dressing. Chill for at least 1 hour before serving. Serve cold.

# Party Spinach Salad

A classic potluck favorite gets a snazzy update! Mango takes the place of canned mandarin oranges, and wasabi-flavored peas offer a fun surprise.

Prep Time: 10 minutes
Cook Time: 5 minutes
Makes 6 servings

Two 3 oz (85 g) packages ramen noodles
1 cup (80 g) slivered almonds
½ lb (250 g) baby spinach, washed
½ lb (250 g) broccoli coleslaw
½ cup (40 g) wasabi-flavored peas
4 tablespoons roughly chopped candied ginger
1 mango, pitted, peeled and cut into thin slices
1 red bell pepper, deseeded and cut into thin strips
4 green onions (scallions), thinly sliced
¾ cup (185 ml) Sesame Dressing (page 28)

Preheat an oven to 350°F (175°C). Crumble the ramen noodles over a baking sheet (discard the seasoning packets). Add the slivered almonds and bake until the almonds just begin to brown (about 5 minutes). Remove from baking sheet and allow to cool a couple of minutes.

In a large serving bowl, toss the baby spinach, broccoli coleslaw, wasabi-flavored peas, candied ginger, mango, red bell pepper, and green onions with the Sesame Dressing.

Just before serving, add the toasted ramen noodles and almonds. Toss well and serve immediately.

Reconstitute seaweed.

Combine dressing ingredients.

Place seaweed and dressing in bowl.

Toss well.

# Seaweed Salad

Did you know that the seaweed salad offered in sushi bars often contains dried fish? If you love seaweed salad but don't eat fish, this salad will help satisfy your cravings.

Prep Time: 15 minutes
Makes 4 servings

3 oz (85 g) dried mixed seaweed
½ cup (125 ml) Amazu Sauce (page 24)
1 tablespoon soy sauce
1 tablespoon sugar
1 teaspoon finely grated fresh ginger
1 tablespoon dark sesame oil
2 teaspoons toasted sesame seeds
2 green onions (scallions), finely sliced
½ teaspoon salt

Reconstitute the seaweed by placing it in a large bowl and covering with lukewarm water. Allow to soak for 10 minutes. Drain the seaweed and squeeze out any excess water.

Stir together the Amazu Sauce, soy sauce, sugar, grated ginger, dark sesame oil, sesame seeds, green onions and salt.

Place the seaweed in a medium-sized bowl and pour the Amazu Sauce mixture over it. Toss well.

Serve immediately or store in the refrigerator for up to 3 days.

# Chapter 3

# NIGIRI, GUNKAN-MAKI & INARI

*Nigiri* sushi, *gunkan-maki* and *inari* sushi are different forms of sushi, but they share a common bond. Simplicity is the theme: each features a single or very limited topping and/or filling. Traditionally, these sushi forms are served in pairs.

Nigiri sushi features one topping served over an individual bed of rice. Traditionally, this type of sushi is used to showcase small tastes of the very best seafood, and is often served without an additional garnish. One need not feel that the vegetable version is an inferior substitute. A bite or two of clean-flavored toppings draped over individual nuggets of rice can be just as exciting to the eyes and taste buds when prepared with care and intention. Blanching is often employed to provide the best color and taste. Garnishes and sauces can also be added in judicious amounts to enhance the flavor.

Gunkan-maki (literally "battleship roll") begins, like nigiri sushi, with an individual bed of rice. This is surrounded with an edible seaweed "wall" that holds in loose toppings. For the vegetarian, sticky *natto* fermented soybeans and faux roe are excellent options that even meat eaters will enjoy. Very thin cucumber slices can also be used as a fresh-tasting "wall" to enclose a spicy and tangy filling.

Inari sushi is kind of miraculous in that it does something that almost no other form of sushi can: it survives beautifully after a day or two in the refrigerator. Inari is truly a make-ahead-and-eat-tomorrow kind of sushi. The plump packages are produced by deep-frying tofu to create a crispy skin, which is then simmered in a sweet and savory broth. The result is a deep-brown "envelope" that can be filled with just about anything you can imagine. This tasty skin remains moist, protecting the fillings and sushi rice it encloses from drying out.

# HOW TO MAKE SUSHI WITHOUT A ROLLING MAT

## Nigiri Sushi

Make the balls of rice a uniform shape and size for the best presentation. Use your fingers to eat nigiri sushi. The toppings, rather than the rice, should be dipped into the sauce—the rice will break apart otherwise. The topping side should be flipped upside down onto the tongue so you taste that first.

1) Dip your fingertips lightly in water and splash the water across your palms. Grab a walnut-sized ball (about 2 tablespoons) of Traditional Sushi Rice (page 21).

2) Lightly squeeze the rice into a flat-bottomed rectangular shape. It is helpful to use your thumb and forefinger to shape the sides.

3) Use kitchen shears to cut a 4 x 7-in (10 x 18-cm) sheet of nori into 12 strips.

4) Drape the desired toppings over the bed of rice.

5) Secure the toppings in place by wrapping one nori "seatbelt" around the center.

Wet fingers and form rice into balls.

Cut the nori into thin "seatbelts."

Drape desired toppings over the rice.

Tuck nori "seatbelts" under the rice.

## Gunkan-Maki

Keep the rice balls for gunkan-maki uniform in size, too. Chopsticks can be used for eating gunkan-maki if desired, as they don't require as much dexterity. Gunkan-maki can be dipped lightly in soy sauce; the nori should keep the pieces bound together.

1) Shape the rice as for nigiri sushi and place on a flat surface.

2) Cut a 4 x 7-in (10 x 18-cm) nori sheet into 1½ x 5-in (4 x 13-cm) strips.

3) Wrap one strip of nori, rough side facing in, around the bed of rice to form a wall. You can use a single grain of rice to "glue" the edges together if necessary.

4) Place the desired fillings inside the wall. Serve immediately.

Cut the nori into thick strips.

Wrap nori around the bed of rice to form a wall.

Add desired toppings.

Blot pouches to remove excess liquid.

# Inari Sushi

**Inari sushi is finger food that can be eaten in multiple bites. Dipping sauces are not usually used, as the pouches have been simmered in seasoned broth.**

Place inari pouches (seasoned tofu pouches) onto a clean, lint-free dish towel or paper towel. Gently blot to remove the excess liquid. Flip the pouches over and blot again. Gently open each pouch, being careful not to tear it.

Carefully open pouches.

## Inari Sushi With Toppings

Wet your fingertips with cool water. Shape 6 tablespoons of Traditional Sushi Rice (page 21), Brown Sushi Rice (page 23), Quinoa Sushi "Rice" (page 22) or Multi-Grain Sushi Rice (page 23) into a small, rectangular bed for each pouch.

Gently slide the rice bed into the pouch. It helps to wiggle the rice in rather than push it.

Flatten the bed of rice with wet fingertips or a wet spoon. The filled inari sushi should stand without tipping over. Adjust the rice as needed. Do not fill the pouches to the top.

Place desired fillings on top of the rice. Serve immediately.

## Stuffed Inari Sushi

Place Traditional Sushi Rice (page 21), Brown Sushi Rice (page 23), Quinoa Sushi "Rice" (page 22) or Multi-Grain Sushi Rice (page 22) in a small bowl. Add additional ingredients as desired. Gently toss with a wet spoon.

Fill each inari pouch with 6 tablespoons of the rice mixture. Gently pack the mixture securely into the pouches.

Fold the edges of the pouches over the fillings and turn over. Serve immediately.

Spoon in the mixed rice.

Fold edges over fillings and turn over.

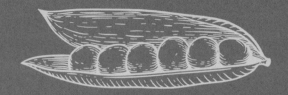

# Vegetable Inari Sushi

Most types of sushi do not fare well after a day of refrigeration. These inari pouches are an exception. The sushi rice is mixed with a flavorful sauce, then completely concealed inside moist tofu-skin pouches. This minimizes the usual drying that occurs when sushi rice is refrigerated.

Rice Prep Time: Up to 1½ hours
Sushi Prep Time: 15 minutes
Makes 8 inari-sushi pouches

2 cups (350 ml) Traditional Sushi Rice, Brown Sushi Rice, Quinoa Sushi "Rice" or Multi-Grain Sushi Rice (pages 21–23)
½ cup (125 ml) Black Bean Sauce (page 25)
2 green onions (scallions), thinly sliced
8 snow peas, roughly chopped
1 small carrot, peeled and shredded
8 inari pouches (seasoned tofu pouches)

Place the rice in a medium-sized bowl. Add the Black Bean Sauce, green onions, snow peas, and carrots. Mix well.

Lay the inari pouches on a clean, lint-free kitchen towel or paper towel and blot away excess liquid.

Carefully open each pouch. Use a wet spoon to add 6 tablespoons of the rice mixture to each pouch. Pack the mixture securely into each pouch. Fold the edges of the pouches over the rice. Turn over and serve.

# Pickled Eggplant Inari Sushi

If you don't have the time to make Miso-Pickled Eggplant, you can still enjoy this sushi. Roasted or grilled eggplant with neutral seasonings makes a good substitute.

Rice Prep Time: Up to 1½ hours
Sushi Prep Time: 15 minutes
Makes 8 inari-sushi pouches

1 teaspoon wakame
2 cups (350 g) Traditional Sushi Rice, Brown Sushi Rice, Quinoa Sushi "Rice" or Multi-Grain Sushi Rice (pages 21–23)
½ cup (150 ml) Miso Dressing (page 24)
1 cup (140 g) Miso-Pickled Eggplant (page 50), diced
8 inari pouches (seasoned tofu pouches)

Place the wakame in a small bowl covered with cold water. Let stand for 5 minutes, or until the wakame has become soft and pliable. Drain well and chop coarsely.

In a medium-sized bowl, mix together the sushi rice, Miso Dressing, Miso-Pickled Eggplant and chopped wakame.

Lay the inari pouches on a clean, lint-free kitchen towel or paper towel and blot away excess liquid.

Carefully open each pouch. Add 6 tablespoons of the rice mixture to each pouch with a wet spoon. Use the spoon to pack the mixture securely into each pouch. Fold the edges of the pouches over the rice.

Turn over and serve.

# Adzuki Bean and Fragrant Herb Inari Sushi

Japanese red bean paste (*anko*) comes in two forms: *koshi-an* and *tsubu-an*. Koshi-an is smooth and free of bean skins. Tsubu-an is chunky and textured. Although both have the same flavor, I recommend the chunkier tsubu-an for this dish.

Rice Prep Time: Up to 1½ hours
Sushi Prep Time: 15 minutes
Makes 8 inari-sushi pouches

2 cups (350 g) Traditional Sushi Rice, Brown Sushi Rice, Quinoa Sushi "Rice" or Multi-Grain Sushi Rice (pages 21-23)
2 tablespoons red bean paste (*anko*)
4 shiso leaves or large sweet basil leaves, chopped
4 large mint leaves, chopped
4 green onions (scallions), thinly sliced
2 teaspoons toasted white sesame seeds
8 inari pouches (seasoned tofu pouches)
2 teaspoons Basic Furikake Seasoning (page 30), or more, to taste

Place the sushi rice in a medium-sized bowl. Add the red bean paste, shiso or sweet basil, mint, green onions and toasted white sesame seeds.

Lay the inari pouches on a clean, lint-free kitchen towel or paper towel and blot away excess liquid.

Carefully open each pouch. Use a damp spoon to scoop 6 tablespoons of the rice mixture into each pouch, packing the mixture in securely.

Sprinkle ¼ teaspoon of the furikake over the filling in each pouch. Fold the edges of the pouches over the rice.

Turn over and serve.

# Shiitake Nigiri

Shiitake are just one type of mushroom that works well for these morsels. Try a bundle of delicate *enoki* mushrooms for a subtler flavor, or robust *shimeji* mushrooms for a stronger flavor.

**Rice Prep Time: Up to 1½ hours**
**Sushi Prep Time: 15 minutes**
**Makes 8 pieces**

8 small shiitake mushrooms, wiped and stems removed
Oil for cooking
One 4 x 7-in (10 x 18-cm) nori sheet
1½ cups (300 g) Traditional Sushi Rice or Brown Sushi Rice (pages 21 and 23)
Tomato Furikake (page 30), to taste
1 teaspoon finely grated fresh ginger
1 green onion (scallion), thinly sliced

Score the top of each mushroom with a knife. Coat the bottom of a large skillet with oil over medium heat. Add the mushrooms and cook just enough to release the fragrance. This should take a couple of minutes. Remove from the skillet and allow to cool.

Cut the sheet of nori crosswise into 8 strips.

Dip your fingertips in water and splash some across your palms. Squeeze a walnut-sized ball of the sushi rice, about 2 tablespoons, in your hand to form a neat rectangular bed of rice. Repeat to make 8 beds of rice in all.

Top each bed of rice with a mushroom. For variety, place half of the mushrooms on the rice beds upside down. Secure the mushrooms in place with a nori strip "seatbelt."

Arrange the pieces on a serving dish. Top each piece with Tomato Furikake, grated ginger and sliced green onion. Serve immediately.

# Sprouts Nigiri

Though not necessary, taking the time to turn all of the sprouts in the same direction makes for the prettiest sushi. To add a little more flavor, tie a chive or piece of green onion (scallion) around the center of the sushi rather than nori to hold the sprouts in place.

**Rice Prep Time: Up to 1½ hours**
**Sushi Prep Time: 15 minutes**
**Makes 12 pieces**

8 oz (250 g) daikon sprouts (*kaiware*) or pea sprouts
One 4 x 7-in (10 x 18-cm) nori sheet
1½ cups (300 g) Traditional Sushi Rice or Brown Sushi Rice (pages 21 and 23)
Ginger Scallion Oil (page 28), to taste

Bring 4 cups (1 liter) of water to a boil in a medium saucepan. Add the daikon sprouts and blanch for 30 seconds. Drain immediately and place in a bowl of ice water.

Cut the sheet of nori crosswise into 12 strips.

Dip your fingertips in water and splash some across your palms. Squeeze a walnut-sized ball of the sushi rice, about 2 tablespoons, in your hand to form a neat rectangular bed of rice. Repeat to make 12 beds of rice in all.

Drain the daikon sprouts and pat dry. Form into 12 small piles.

Top each bed of rice with some of the sprouts. Secure the daikon sprouts in place with a nori strip "seatbelt."

Drizzle Ginger Scallion Oil over the pieces, to taste.

# Spicy Carrot and Tomato Inari Sushi

When preparing a spicy mixture such as the carrots featured in this dish, I like to use two types of chili sauces. The combination of the two makes the mixture balanced with an overall heat profile that doesn't taste like either of the individual sauces.

Rice Prep Time: Up to 1½ hours
Sushi Prep Time: 15 minutes
Makes 6 pieces

1 carrot, finely diced
1 tablespoon sriracha
1 tablespoon garlic chili paste
1 teaspoon Chia Seed
  Togarashi (page 28) or
  shichimi togarashi (seven-
  flavor pepper), plus more for
  topping
1 teaspoon toasted sesame
  seeds
1 green onion (scallion),
  thinly sliced
⅛ teaspoon dark sesame oil
½ teaspoon salt
2 cups (350 ml) Traditional
  Sushi Rice, Brown Sushi
  Rice, Quinoa Sushi "Rice"
  or Multi-Grain Sushi Rice
  (pages 21–23)
8 inari pouches (seasoned tofu
  pouches)
12 cherry tomatoes, halved

In a bowl, toss together the carrot, sriracha, garlic chili paste, Chia Seed Togarashi, sesame seeds, green onion, dark sesame oil, salt and sushi rice.

Lay the inari pouches on a clean, lint-free kitchen towel or paper towel and blot away excess liquid.

Carefully open each pouch. Use a wet spoon to add 6 tablespoons of the rice mixture to each pouch, packing the mixture in securely.

Arrange the inari pouches on a serving tray. Add four cherry tomato halves and sprinkle with Chia Seed Togarashi, to taste.

# Tamago Nigiri

**The use of crepe-like omelette sheets cuts the preparation time in half but delivers the same flavor as that of a traditional Japanese rolled omelette log. Try sprinkling each piece with Basic, Tomato or Curry Furikake Seasoning (page 30).**

**Rice Prep Time: Up to 1½ hours**
**Sushi Prep Time: 15 minutes**
**Makes about 12 pieces**

12 Japanese Omelette Sheets
One 4 x 7-in (10 x 18-cm) nori
   sheet
1½ cups (300 g) Traditional Sushi
   Rice or Brown Sushi Rice (pages 21
   and 23)

Cut each omelette into matchstick-thin strips. Cut the sheet of nori crosswise into 12 strips.

Dip your fingertips in water and splash some across your palms. Squeeze a walnut-sized ball of the sushi rice, about 2 tablespoons, in your hand to form a neat rectangular bed of rice. Repeat to make 12 beds of rice in all.

Divide the omelette into 12 piles.

Top each bed of rice with a heap of the omelette strips. Wrap a strip of nori around each piece of rice to secure the omelette strips in place.

## Japanese Omelette Sheets

**Prep Time: 5 minutes**
**Cook Time: 15 minutes**
**Makes 12 sheets**

5 large eggs
4 tablespoons Vegetarian Dashi
   (page 27) or low-sodium
   vegetable stock, cooled 1
   tablespoon sugar
2 tablespoons soy sauce
½ teaspoon salt
Oil for frying

Whisk the eggs, Vegetarian Dashi or vegetable stock, sugar, soy sauce and salt together in a medium bowl. Pass the mixture through a fine-mesh strainer to eliminate small bits. Heat a skillet over medium heat. Wad a large paper towel into a ball and dip it into some cooking oil. Use chopsticks or tongs to rub the paper towel around the skillet.

Add ½ cup (125 ml) of the egg mixture to the oiled skillet. Tilt the skillet to coat the bottom. When the egg has set, loosen the edges with a pair of chopsticks. Flip the omelette onto a plate.

Repeat the steps with the remaining egg mixture. (Place omelettes on separate plates for cooling purposes.)

Strain the egg mixture.

# Spinach Nigiri

I prefer bundled spinach to bagged spinach for this preparation. Keep the spinach leaves turned in the same direction when cooking for the prettiest nigiri.

Lightly oil the skillet.

Cook until set and lightly browned underneath.

Transfer the omelette onto a plate to cool.

Rice Prep Time: Up to 1½ hours
Sushi Prep Time: 15 minutes
Makes 12 pieces

8 oz (250 g) fresh spinach
    leaves, trimmed of stems
½ cup (125 ml) water
½ teaspoon dark sesame oil
Pinch of salt
1½ cups (300 g) Traditional
    Sushi Rice or Brown Sushi
    Rice (pages 21 and 23)
1 teaspoon black sesame
    seeds

In a microwave-safe bowl, mix the spinach, water, dark sesame oil and salt. Cover with plastic wrap and microwave on high for 30 seconds. Remove the spinach and give it a good squeeze to remove as much liquid as possible.

Dip your fingertips in water and splash some across your palms. Squeeze a walnut-sized ball of the sushi rice, about 2 tablespoons, in your hand to form a neat rectangular bed of rice. Repeat to make 12 beds of rice in all.

Top each bed of rice with some of the wilted spinach.

Sprinkle with black sesame seeds before serving.

# Faux Roe "Boats"

Cooked amaranth has a very similar texture to *masago* (capelin fish roe). The kombu kelp adds a fresh ocean flavor. Prepare only enough Faux Roe to use in one sushi-making session, as leftovers tend to become gelatinous and unpleasant in texture.

Rice Prep Time: Up to 1½ hours
Sushi Prep Time: 15 minutes
Makes 12 pieces

1½ cups (300 g) Traditional Sushi
  Rice or Brown Sushi Rice (pages 21
  and 23)
Six 4 x 7-in (10 x 18-cm) nori sheets
½ cup (130 g) Faux Roe

Wet your fingertips and palms lightly with water. Grab a walnut-sized amount of the sushi rice (about 2 tablespoons) and mold it into a rectangular mound. The bottom should be flat. Repeat this with the remaining rice to form 12 "beds" in all.

Cut the nori into twelve 1½ x 5-in (4 x 13-cm) strips. (Any remaining nori can be saved and cut into "seatbelts" for nigiri sushi.) Wrap one strip of nori, rough side facing in, around 1 bed of rice to form a wall. If desired, use a single grain of rice to "glue" the edges together. Repeat with remaining nori strips and rice beds.

Arrange the rice beds on a serving tray. Top each with 1 tablespoon of the Faux Roe.

Prepare 12 rice "beds."

Cut nori into 12 strips.

Wrap 1 strip of nori around each bed of rice.

Place 1 Tbsp Faux Roe on top of each bed of rice.

## Faux Roe

A small amount of turmeric adds a vibrant yellow hue without overpowering the flavor.

Prep Time: 5 minutes
Cook Time: 20 minutes

1½ cups (375 ml) Vegetarian
  Dashi (page 27) or low-sodium
  vegetable broth
½ cup (100 g) amaranth
½ teaspoon salt
¼ teaspoon turmeric
One ½-in (1.25-cm) piece kombu
  (kelp), wiped with a damp cloth

Bring the Vegetarian Dashi to a boil in a medium saucepan. Add the amaranth, salt, and turmeric, stirring well to prevent sticking. Add the kombu. Cover the pan and reduce heat to keep at a low simmer. Cook for 20 minutes. There should still be some liquid left in the pan. Strain the amaranth and set aside to cool.

## Variation
### Wasabi Faux Roe
Omit turmeric. Cook amaranth and drain as described above. Mix 1 teaspoon of wasabi powder in 1 tablespoon of water. Toss the amaranth with the wasabi mixture and 1 or more drops green food coloring (optional). Cool before using.

# Cucumber and Peanut "Boats"

The use of a mandoline is key for these little boats, as the cucumber needs to be sliced very thin so it wraps easily. If your cucumber is too thick, you can use a length of green onion or chive to "tie" it into place.

Rice Prep Time: 1½ hours
Sushi Prep Time: 15 minutes
Makes 12 pieces

1½ cups (300 g) Traditional
  Sushi Rice or Brown Sushi
  Rice (pages 21 and 23)
1 English cucumber
½ cup (40 g) roasted peanuts
1 teaspoon finely grated
  daikon radish
1 teaspoon grated ginger root
Chia Seed Togarashi (page 28)
  or shichimi togarashi
One green onion (scallion),
  thinly sliced
Sweet Chili Sauce (page 25), for
  dipping

Wet your fingertips and palms lightly with water. Grab a walnut-sized amount of prepared sushi rice (about 2 tablespoons) and mold it into a rectangular mound. The bottom should be flat. Repeat this with the remaining rice to form 12 balls in all.

Use a mandoline to cut the cucumber lengthwise into very thin slices. (Eat the first slice or two, as they will most likely not be long or wide enough.) The slices must be wide enough to extend above the height of the rice balls when wrapped around them like a wall. You should be able to get 6 slices from one side of the cucumber. Avoid using the middle slices that are full of seeds. Turn the cucumber over to get 6 more slices from the other side.

Wrap a cucumber slice snugly around each rice ball to enclose it in a wall. The ends should stick to each other. Place an equal quantity of peanuts on top of each rice ball. Add a tiny dab of grated daikon radish and a tiny dab of grated ginger root on top of the peanuts. Sprinkle with Chia Seed Togarashi or shichimi togarashi and top with green onion.

Dip the bottoms of the little boats in Sweet Chili Sauce before eating.

# Baby Bok Choy Nigiri with Black Bean Sauce

Select baby bok choy that are finger length or shorter. If baby bok choy are unavailable, cut standard bok choy into 1 x 2-inch (2.5 x 5-cm) pieces.

**Rice Prep Time: Up to 1½ hours**
**Sushi Prep Time: 15 minutes**
**Makes 12 pieces**

**6 heads baby bok choy**
**One 4 x 7-in (10 x 18-cm) sheet of nori**
**1½ cups (300 g) Traditional Sushi Rice or Brown Sushi Rice (pages 21 and 23)**
**6 teaspoons Black Bean Sauce (page 25)**
**2 tablespoons fresh orange zest, or more, to taste**

Bring 4 cups (1 liter) of water to a boil in a medium saucepan. Add the baby bok choy and blanch for 1 minute. Drain immediately and rinse in cold water.

Slice the baby bok choy in half lengthwise. Pat dry with a clean, lint-free kitchen towel or paper towel.

Cut the sheet of nori crosswise into 12 strips.

Dip your fingertips in water and splash some across your palms. Squeeze a walnut-sized ball of prepared Sushi Rice, about 2 tablespoons, in your hand to form a neat rectangular bed of rice. Repeat to make 12 beds of rice in all.

Lay one baby bok choy half (cut side down) on each of the rice beds. Secure the boy choy in place with a nori strip "seatbelt."

To serve, arrange the pieces on a serving dish. Spoon ½ teaspoon of the Black Bean Sauce over each piece and sprinkle with orange zest.

Cover the vegetables with salt.

# Broccoli-Stem Kimchi Inari

**I prefer to use the stems of the broccoli to the florets. These bites are ready in just minutes and can be refrigerated for up to a week.**

Toss with chili paste and ginger.

Rice Prep Time: 1½ hours
Sushi Prep Time: 25 minutes
Makes 8 pieces

8 inari pouches (seasoned tofu pouches)
2 cups (350 g) prepared Traditional Sushi
   Rice, Brown Sushi Rice, Quinoa Sushi
   "Rice" or Multi-Grain Sushi Rice (pages
   21–23)
1 cup (200 g) Broccoli-Stem Kimchi

**Broccoli-Stem Kimchi**
One 4-in (10-cm) length broccoli stem, sliced
One 2-in (5-cm) length daikon radish,
   peeled and thinly sliced
1 carrot, shredded
2 green onions (scallions), roughly chopped
4 tablespoons salt
2 tablespoons garlic chili paste
1 teaspoon grated fresh ginger root

Prepare the Broccoli-Stem Kimchi: Toss the broccoli stem, daikon radish, carrot and green onions in a bowl with the salt. Let stand for 10 minutes, then rinse thoroughly. Squeeze the excess water out.

Mix the vegetables with garlic chili paste and ginger. Let stand for 5 minutes for flavors to develop.

Lay the inari pouches on a clean, lint-free kitchen towel or paper towel and blot away excess liquid.

Carefully open each pouch. Use a wet spoon to scoop 6 tablespoons of sushi rice into each pouch, packing it in securely.

Pour off the excess liquid from the kimchi. You can save the liquid to make more broccoli-stem kimchi or discard it.

Divide the kimchi evenly across the tops of the 6 packets. Serve immediately.

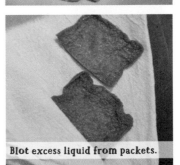
Blot excess liquid from packets.

Fill each packet with sushi rice.

Top each packet with kimchi.

# Chapter 4

# THIN SUSHI ROLLS

It may take a few attempts to master this classic sushi rolling technique. At the heart of mastery is self-control. Each roll is made with a single choice ingredient that either stands alone or is enhanced with a dab of sauce, a pinch of herbs, or a sprinkling of nuts. Though it's often tempting to add just one more filling, doing so can result in a roll that refuses to seal or that pops open in the most unexpected places.

Another common temptation is to moisten the loose flap of nori with water before cutting the roll into pieces. Instead, allow the sushi roll to sit undisturbed on your cutting board for up to 2 minutes. Moisture from the sushi rice will gradually seep through the nori and seal the flap properly. When excess water is added, the seal will release as the nori becomes slick from the absorbed moisture.

Enjoy thin sushi rolls shortly after preparation. The nori on the outside of the roll will continue to absorb moisture from the rice, causing the wrapper to become quite chewy. The nori will toughen further if the sushi rolls are refrigerated for more than an hour. If you need to prepare the rolls ahead of time, substitute soy paper for the nori.

# HOW TO MAKE THIN SUSHI ROLLS

1) Arrange a bamboo rolling mat so that the slats run parallel to the work surface. Begin with a 4 x 7-in (10 x 18-cm) sheet of nori. Place the nori on the mat so that the long end is parallel to the bottom of the mat. The rough side of the nori should face upwards.

2) Dip your fingertips in cool water. Spread about ½ cup (100 g) of prepared sushi rice evenly over the bottom ¾ of the nori sheet. (The amount of rice needed tends to lessen with practice.)

3) Arrange the fillings in a thin line extending to the edges of the nori. For best results, use no more than two substantial vegetable fillings and one light one such as sesame seeds or a sauce.

4) Wet your fingertips again. Place your thumbs underneath the bamboo rolling mat while grasping the fillings with your fingertips. Fold the bottom edge of the mat so that the nori fits just over the fillings. Do not allow the edge of the bamboo rolling mat to get stuck inside the fold.

5) Gently lift the edge of the mat. (You should be able to see a strip of nori that is not covered with rice.) Continue rolling until the seam is on the bottom edge of the roll. Gently shape the roll into a rectangle by pressing your forefingers on the top of the mat while simultaneously pressing your thumbs and middle fingers on the sides.

6) Remove the completed roll from the mat. There may be a small flap of nori that is not completely sealed. Do not wet with water to seal. Simply allow the roll to rest seam-side down on a cutting board for about 2 minutes.

7) Dip the tip of a very sharp knife into a small bowl of water. Tap the knife heel on the cutting surface so that the water runs down the length of the blade. Cut the roll into 6 pieces using a swift sawing motion, re-dipping the knife tip as needed.

Place nori horizontally on mat, rough side up.

Spread rice evenly across the bottom ¾ of nori.

Arrange fillings across the center of the rice.

Fold bottom edge of mat so nori folds over fillings.

Set completed roll seam-side down for 2 minutes.

Cut roll into 6 pieces with a water-dipped knife.

# Apple Daikon Rolls

**Crisp Granny Smith apples and daikon make a lovely pair. Depending on your personal preference, the apple can be peeled or unpeeled. To keep the apple from browning, toss with a little rice vinegar. Just be sure to pat the pieces completely dry before adding to the sushi roll.**

**Rice Prep Time: Up to 1½ hours (note that Vegetarian Ponzu Sauce must be prepared a day ahead)**
**Sushi Prep Time: 15 minutes**
**Makes 4 rolls (24 pieces)**

Four 4 x 7-in (10 x 18-cm) nori sheets
2 cups (350 g) Traditional Sushi Rice, Brown Sushi Rice, Quinoa Sushi Rice or Multi-Grain Sushi Rice (pages 21–23)
4 tablespoons Chili Daikon (page 31), drained
½ Granny Smith apple, cored and cut into matchsticks
2 green onions (scallions), sliced
Vegetarian Ponzu Sauce (page 26) for dipping

Place one nori sheet horizontally on a bamboo rolling mat, rough side facing upwards. Wet your fingertips and spread ¼ of the rice in a thin, even layer across the bottom ¾ of the nori.

Smear 1 tablespoon of the Chili Daikon across the center of the rice. Arrange ¼ of the Granny Smith apple sticks horizontally in the center of the rice, extending to both sides of the nori. Sprinkle ¼ of the green onions across the center.

Dip your fingertips in water again. Place your thumbs underneath the bamboo rolling mat. Fold the bottom of the mat so that the bottom edge of the nori fits just over the apple. (Do not allow the edge of the mat to get stuck in the fold!)

Lift the edge of the mat. (The nori should stay in place.) Continue rolling until the roll is complete. Gently shape the roll into a rectangle by pressing your forefingers on top of the mat while simultaneously pressing your thumbs and middle fingers into the sides.

Allow the roll to rest seam-side down on a cutting board. Meanwhile, repeat the steps to complete the remaining rolls. Cut each roll into 6 pieces using a very sharp knife dipped lightly in water. Serve immediately with Vegetarian Ponzu Sauce, if desired.

# Cucumber Rolls

**Japanese or English cucumbers may seem like a splurge, but they are definitely worth it for these single-feature rolls. If using garden cucumbers, peel away the bitter skins before cutting into small pieces.**

Rice Prep Time: Up to 1½ hours
Sushi Prep Time: 15 minutes
Makes 4 rolls (24 pieces)

Four 4 x 7-in (10 x 18-cm) nori sheets
2 cups (400 g) Traditional Sushi Rice, Brown Sushi Rice, Quinoa Sushi "Rice" or Multi-Grain Sushi Rice (pages 21–23)
2 Japanese cucumbers or 1 English cucumber, deseeded and cut into 4-in (10-cm) matchsticks
1 teaspoon toasted sesame seeds

Place one nori sheet horizontally on a bamboo rolling mat, rough side facing upwards. Wet your fingertips, then spread about ½ cup (100 g) of the sushi rice in a thin, even layer across the bottom ¾ of the nori.

Arrange ¼ of the cucumber sticks horizontally across the center of the rice. The cucumber should extend to the edges of the nori. Sprinkle ¼ teaspoon of sesame seeds over the rice.

Dip your fingertips in water again. Place your thumbs underneath the bamboo rolling mat. Fold the bottom of the mat so that the bottom edge of the nori fits just over the cucumbers. (Do not allow the edge of the mat to get stuck in the fold!)

Lift the edge of the mat. (The nori should stay in place.) Continue rolling until the roll is complete. Gently shape the roll into a rectangle by pressing your forefingers on top of the mat while simultaneously pressing your thumbs and middle fingers into the sides.

Allow the roll to rest seam-side down on a cutting board. Meanwhile, repeat the steps to complete the remaining rolls. Cut each roll into 6 pieces using a very sharp knife dipped lightly in water. Serve immediately.

## Variation
### Cucumber Mint Rolls
Begin assembling the rolls as directed. Smear ¼ teaspoon tahini across the rice. Add a few torn fresh mint leaves before topping with cucumbers. Add sesame seeds. Roll and cut as directed. Serve with Vegetarian Ponzu Sauce (Page 26) for dipping.

# Pomegranate and Basil Rolls

If you can't find the pomegranate seeds or arils already prepared, use this easy method to take them from the whole fruit: Slice the pomegranate in half, then break the halves into pieces over a large bowl of water. Working with one piece at a time, continue to break the pieces into smaller ones in the water. Pull the arils away from the pulp. The seeds should sink as the pulp floats. Discard the pulp and store the arils in fresh water in the refrigerator for up to 2 weeks.

Rice Prep Time: Up to 1½ hours
Sushi Prep Time: 15 minutes
Makes 4 rolls (24 pieces)

**Four 4 x 7-in (10 x 18-cm) nori sheets**
**2 cups (400 g) Traditional Sushi Rice, Brown Sushi Rice, Quinoa Sushi "Rice" or Multi-Grain Sushi Rice (pages 21–23)**
**16 large green Greek olives, pitted and quartered lengthwise**
**8 large basil leaves**
**4 tablespoons pomegranate arils, plus more for garnish if desired**

Place one nori sheet horizontally on a bamboo rolling mat with the rough side facing up. Wet your fingertips, then spread about ½ cup (100 g) of the sushi rice in a thin, even layer across the bottom ¾ of the nori.

Arrange ¼ of the Greek olives horizontally in the center of the rice. The olives should extend to the side edges of the nori. Tear 2 basil leaves and spread them across the rice. Arrange 1 tablespoon of the pomegranate arils across the rice, making sure to keep them as close to the center of the rice as possible.

Dip your fingertips in water again. Place your thumbs underneath the bamboo rolling mat. Fold the bottom of the mat so that the bottom edge of the nori fits just over the fillings. (Do not allow the edge of the mat to get stuck in the fold!)

Lift the edge of the mat. (The nori should stay in place.) Continue rolling until the roll is complete. Gently shape the roll into a rectangle by pressing your forefingers on top of the mat while simultaneously pressing your thumbs and middle fingers into the sides.

Allow the roll to rest seam-side down on a cutting board. Meanwhile, repeat the steps to complete the remaining rolls. Cut each roll into 6 pieces using a very sharp knife dipped lightly in water. Serve immediately.

# Sesame Seaweed Rolls

I always have one sheet of nori wrapped in plastic wrap that I store with my sushi supplies. It is my practical measuring guide. When I make this sushi roll, I use my plastic-wrapped piece of nori as a guide for cutting the kombu to the perfect size.

**Rice Prep Time: Up to 1½ hours**
**Sushi Prep Time: 20 minutes**
**Makes 4 rolls (24 pieces)**

4 large pieces of kombu kelp
2 cups (400 g) Traditional Sushi
   Rice, Brown Sushi Rice, Quinoa
   Sushi "Rice" or Multi-Grain Sushi
   Rice (pages 21-23)
4 teaspoons Sesame Dressing (page
   28); more for dipping if desired
Four 7-in (18-cm) pieces *kampyo*
   (simmered gourd)
1 teaspoon toasted sesame seeds

Bring about 4 quarts of water to a near boil. Remove from the heat and add the kombu. Allow to sit for 5 minutes. Remove the kombu and squeeze out excess water.

Cut the kombu into rectangles about 4 x 7 inches (10 x 18 cm).

Place one sheet of kombu horizontally across a bamboo rolling mat. Wet your fingertips, then spread about ½ cup (100 g) of the sushi rice in a thin, even layer across the bottom ¾ of the kombu.

Spread 1 teaspoon of Sesame Dressing across the rice. Arrange 1 piece of kampyo across the rice, extending to both edges. Sprinkle ¼ teaspoon of sesame seeds over the kampyo.

Dip your fingertips in water again. Place your thumbs underneath the bamboo rolling mat. Fold the bottom of the mat so that the bottom edge of the kombu fits just over the kampyo. (Do not allow the edge of the mat to get stuck in the fold!)

Lift the edge of the mat. (The kombu should stay in place.) Continue rolling until the roll is complete. Gently shape the roll into a rectangle by pressing your forefingers on top of the mat while simultaneously pressing your thumbs and middle fingers into the sides.

Place the roll seam-side down on a cutting board. Meanwhile, repeat the steps to complete the remaining rolls. Cut each roll into 6 pieces using a very sharp knife dipped lightly in water. Serve immediately with additional Sesame Dressing, if desired.

Place nori horizontally on rolling mat.

Roll nori over added rice and fillings.

Cut each roll into 6 pieces.

# Asparagus Almond Rolls

**A dull or lightweight knife can sometimes snag on the almonds, pulling rather than cutting them. This can rip the nori and make the slices uneven. To prevent this, make sure your knife is very sharp and exert a little extra force when cutting pieces.**

**Rice Prep Time: Up to 1½ hours**
**Sushi Prep Time: 15 minutes**
**Makes 4 rolls (24 pieces)**

Four 4 x 7-in (10 x 18 cm)
   nori sheets
2 cups (350 g) Traditional
   Sushi Rice, Brown Sushi
   Rice, Quinoa Sushi "Rice"
   or Multi-Grain Sushi Rice
   (pages 21–23)
1 teaspoon Sesame Soy
   Mustard (page 29)
4 teaspoons toasted almond
   slivers, roughly chopped
8 asparagus spears, blanched

Place one sheet of the nori horizontally on a bamboo rolling mat, rough side up. Wet your fingertips, then spread about ½ cup (100 g) of the sushi rice in a thin, even layer across the bottom ¾ of the nori.

Smear ¼ teaspoon of the Sesame Soy Mustard across the center of the rice. Add 1 teaspoon of the almonds across the center. Arrange 2 of the asparagus spears across the center of the rice. The tips should extend past the edges of the nori.

Dip your fingertips in water again. Place your thumbs underneath the bamboo rolling mat. Fold the bottom of the mat so that the bottom edge of the nori fits just over the asparagus spears. (Do not allow the

edge of the mat to get stuck in the fold!) Lift the edge of the mat. (The nori should stay in place.) Continue rolling until the roll is complete. Gently shape the roll into a rectangle by pressing your forefingers on top of the mat while simultaneously pressing your thumbs and middle fingers into the sides.

Allow the roll to rest seam-side down on a cutting board. Meanwhile, repeat the steps to complete the remaining rolls. Cut each roll into 6 pieces using a very sharp knife dipped lightly in water. Serve immediately.

# Traditional Pickled Vegetable Rolls

**Resist the urge to combine different types of pickles inside a single roll. Using just one variety for each roll allows every component—rice, pickle, nori—to be fully appreciated.**

**Rice Prep Time: Up to 1½ hours**
**Sushi Prep Time: 15 minutes**
**Makes 4 rolls (24 pieces)**

**Four 4 x 7-in (10 x 18-cm) nori sheets**
**2 cups (400 g) Traditional Sushi Rice, Brown Sushi Rice, Quinoa Sushi "Rice" or Multi-Grain Sushi Rice (pages 21–23)**
**One 4-in (10-cm) length *takuan* (pickled daikon), cut into sticks**

Place one nori sheet horizontally on a bamboo rolling mat with the rough side facing up. Wet your fingertips, then spread about ½ cup (100 g) of the sushi rice in a thin, even layer across the bottom ¾ of the nori.

Arrange ¼ of the takuan sticks horizontally in the center of the rice. The pickles should extend to the edges of the nori.

Dip your fingertips in water again. Place your thumbs underneath the bamboo rolling mat. Fold the bottom of the mat so that the bottom edge of the nori fits just over the pickles. (Do not allow the edge of the mat to get stuck in the fold!)

Lift the edge of the mat. (The nori should stay in place.) Continue rolling until the roll is complete. Gently shape the roll into a rectangle by pressing your forefingers on top of the mat while simultaneously pressing your thumbs and middle fingers into the sides.

Allow the roll to rest seam-side down on a cutting board. Meanwhile, repeat the steps to complete the remaining rolls. Cut each roll into 6 pieces using a very sharp knife dipped lightly in water. Serve immediately.

## Variation
### Kampyo Rolls
Replace the takuan with two 7-in (18-cm) strips of *kampyo* pickled gourd per sushi roll. Shape and cut as directed above.

## Variation
### Miso-Pickled Eggplant Rolls
Replace the takuan with 2 finger-width lengths of Miso-Pickled Eggplant (page 50) per sushi roll. Shape and cut as directed above.

## Variation
### Lotus Rootlet Rolls
Replace takuan with 2 brined lotus rootlets (available in jars at your local Asian market) per sushi roll. If desired, add thinly sliced green onion (scallion). Roll and cut as directed above.

Strain cooked squash and cool before using.

Spread sushi rice over nori and top with fillings.

Roll nori over the rice and fillings.

# Butternut Squash Rolls

**Creamy butternut squash pairs well with sweet and spicy crystallized ginger. If, like me, you're particularly fond of crystallized ginger, provide some on the side in place of pickled ginger as a palate cleanser.**

**Rice Prep Time: Up to 1½ hours**
**Sushi Prep Time: 30 minutes**
**Makes 6 rolls (36 pieces)**

8 oz (250 g) butternut squash, peeled and deseeded
2½ cups (635 ml) Vegetarian Dashi (page 27) or low-sodium vegetable stock
2 cloves garlic
One 1-in (1.25-cm) length fresh ginger, unpeeled
4 tablespoons soy sauce
Six 4 x 7-in (10 x 18-cm) nori sheets
3 cups (600 g) Traditional Sushi Rice, Brown Sushi Rice, Quinoa Sushi "Rice" or Multi-Grain Sushi Rice (pages 21–23)
3 teaspoons finely chopped crystallized ginger
3 green onions (scallions), sliced
Vegetarian Eel Sauce (page 26) for dipping, if desired

Cut the squash into 12 strips about 4 x ½ in (10 x 1.25 cm) and set aside. Combine the Vegetarian Dashi, garlic, and fresh ginger in a small pot. Bring to a rapid boil over high heat. Reduce to a simmer and add the soy sauce. Place the squash in a wire basket or strainer and lower into the simmering liquid. Allow the squash to simmer until soft but not mushy, 5–7 minutes. Remove squash from liquid and allow to cool completely.

Place one nori sheet horizontally on a bamboo rolling mat with the rough side facing up. Wet your fingertips, then spread about ½ cup (100 g) of the sushi rice in a thin, even layer across the bottom ¾ of the nori.

Arrange 2 of the butternut squash sticks horizontally across the center of the rice. It's okay if the ends overlap some in the center. Sprinkle ½ teaspoon crystallized ginger over the top. Add ¼

of the green onions.

Dip your fingertips in water again. Place your thumbs underneath the bamboo rolling mat. Fold the bottom of the mat so that the bottom edge of the nori fits just over the butternut. (Do not allow the edge of the mat to get stuck in the fold!)

Lift the edge of the mat. (The nori should stay in place.) Continue rolling until the roll is complete. Gently shape the roll into a rectangle by pressing your forefingers on top of the mat while simultaneously pressing your thumbs and middle fingers into the sides.

Allow the roll to rest seam-side down on a cutting board. Meanwhile, repeat the steps to complete the remaining rolls. Cut each roll into 6 pieces using a very sharp knife dipped lightly in water. Serve immediately.

# Chapter 5

# THICK SUSHI ROLLS

When I teach sushi classes, I always start with *futo-maki*, or thick rolls. They are the easiest to master within the eager first or second attempt. Using the nori vertically allows a greater number of fillings to be contained in a manageable bite. The hardest part of preparing thick rolls may be deciding when to stop adding fillings. The good news is that even if you get a little carried away, you'll still end up with good results. And don't worry about fillings sticking out of the ends. In fact, you'll achieve better results if your fillings stick out, because they'll provide valuable structure when cutting the roll into pieces. Like thin sushi rolls, thick sushi rolls should be enjoyed shortly after preparation. Soybean paper can be used if rolls need to be prepared in advance.

Thick sushi rolls like Coconut Tempura Tofu Rolls and Mushroom "Spider" Rolls offer a great way to incorporate crispy fried elements without having to fry the entire roll. The warm and crunchy fried fillings offer a pleasing contrast to the cool vegetables and perfectly cooked sushi rice, enhancing the overall sushi experience.

# HOW TO MAKE THICK SUSHI ROLLS

1) Place a 4 x 7-in (10 x 18-cm) sheet of nori vertically on a bamboo rolling mat. Make sure that the short end is parallel to the bottom of the mat and that the rough side is facing upwards.

2) Dip your fingertips lightly in cool water and spread about ¾ cup (150 g) of prepared sushi rice evenly over the bottom ¾ of the nori.

3) Add the desired fillings horizontally across the middle of the rice, making sure that the fillings extend to both edges of the nori. For best results, use at least 3 fillings, but no more than 7.

4) Wet your fingertips again and slide your thumbs underneath the mat while grasping the fillings with all other fingertips. Roll the bottom of the mat just over the fillings, tucking the fillings tightly under the fold. (Do not allow the mat to get stuck inside the roll!)

Lift the edge of the mat. Continue rolling until the roll is complete and the seam is facing down. Gently shape the roll by pressing your forefingers on top of the mat while simultaneously pressing your thumbs and middle fingers on the sides.

5) Allow the roll to rest seam-side down on a cutting board for at least 2 minutes. A loose fold is common with thick rolls, but resist the urge to seal with additional water. The moisture from the sushi rice will be sufficient for the nori to adhere to itself.

6) To cut the roll, dip the blade of a very sharp knife in water. Use a swift sawing motion to cut the roll into 5 pieces.

Place nori vertically on the mat, rough side up.

Spread rice evenly across the bottom ¾ of nori.

Arrange fillings across the center of the rice.

Fold the bottom edge of the nori to cover fillings.

Set roll seam-side down for 2 minutes.

Cut roll into 5 pieces with a water-dipped knife.

# Spicy Tofu Rolls

**Many sushi bars like to add spicy mayonnaise to their fillings, but I prefer to add it to the tops of rolls, where it stays tidy. Adding it to the mix makes things messy, as the mayonnaise often oozes out the sides during the rolling process.**

Rice Prep Time: Up to 1½ hours
Sushi Prep Time: 20 minutes
Makes 4 rolls (20 pieces)

4 oz (100 g) tofu, drained
  and cut into tiny cubes
1 green onion (scallion),
  thinly sliced
1 tablespoon fresh orange
  juice
½ teaspoon fresh orange zest
1 teaspoon Chia Seed
  Togarashi (page 28)
  or *shichimi togarashi*
  (Japanese 7-flavor pepper)
1 teaspoon dark sesame oil
1 tablespoon garlic chili
  paste
Salt, to taste
Four 4 x 7-in (10 x 18-cm)
  nori sheets
3 cups (600 g) Traditional
  Sushi Rice, Brown Sushi
  Rice, Quinoa Sushi "Rice"
  or Multi-Grain Sushi Rice
  (pages 21–23)
¼ avocado, cut into 4
  wedges
One 4-in (10-cm) length
  carrot, cut into matchsticks
Curry Mayonnaise (page 29),
  to taste
Faux Roe (page 68)

Mix together the tofu, green onion, orange juice, fresh orange zest, Chia Seed Togarashi, dark sesame oil, and garlic chili paste. Add salt, to taste.

Place a 4 x 7-in (10 x 18-cm) sheet of nori vertically on a bamboo rolling mat. Make sure that the short end is parallel to the bottom of the mat and that the rough side is facing upwards.

Dip your fingertips lightly in cool water and spread about ¾ cup (150 g) of the sushi rice evenly over the bottom ¾ of the nori.

Spread 2½ tablespoons of the spicy tofu mixture horizontally across the center of the rice. Place 1 avocado wedge on top of the spicy tofu. Top with ¼ of the carrots.

Wet your fingertips again and slide your thumbs underneath the mat while grasping the fillings with all other fingertips. Roll the bottom of the mat just over the fillings, tucking the fillings tightly under the fold. (Do not allow the mat to get stuck inside the roll!)

Lift the edge of the mat. Continue rolling until the roll is complete and the seam is facing down. Gently shape the roll by pressing your forefingers on top of the mat while simultaneously pressing your thumbs and middle fingers on the sides.

Allow the roll to rest seam-side down on a cutting board for at least 2 minutes. Repeat steps to make 3 more rolls.

To cut the rolls, dip the blade of a very sharp knife in water. Use a swift sawing motion to cut each roll into 5 pieces. Dollop Curry Mayonnaise on each piece as desired before serving.

# Ginger Beet Rolls

**Tossing a bit of grated beet with the sushi rice gives it a pleasant pink hue and prevents your rolls from looking as if they are bleeding. Regardless of the type of beet you use, be sure to mix some of it with your sushi rice before making the rolls for the best presentation.**

**Rice Prep Time: Up to 1½ hours (note that Ponzu Sauce should be made a day ahead)**
**Sushi Prep Time: 15 minutes**
**Makes 4 rolls (20 pieces)**

**3 cups (600 g) Traditional Sushi Rice, Brown Sushi Rice, Quinoa Sushi "Rice" or Multi-Grain Sushi Rice (pages 21–23)**
**½ teaspoon grated raw beet**
**Four 4 x 7-in (10 x 18-cm) nori sheets**
**2 teaspoons grated fresh ginger**
**1 teaspoon lemon zest**
**1 large beet, roasted, peeled and cut into thin strips**
**½ carrot, peeled and cut into matchsticks**
**1 bunch watercress, trimmed**
**Vegetarian Ponzu Sauce (page 26) for dipping**

Toss the grated beet and sushi rice together until the mixture turns pink.

Place a 4 x 7-inch (10 x 18-cm) sheet of nori vertically on a bamboo rolling mat. Make sure that the short end is parallel to the bottom of the mat and that the rough side is facing upwards.

Dip your fingertips lightly in cool water and spread about ¾ cup (150 g) of the pinkened sushi rice evenly over the bottom ¾ of the nori.

Smear ½ teaspoon of the grated ginger across the center of the rice. Sprinkle ¼ teaspoon of the lemon zest over the rice. Arrange ¼ of the roasted beet, carrot, and watercress horizontally across the middle of the rice, making sure that the fillings extend to both edges of the nori.

Wet your fingertips again and slide your thumbs underneath the mat while grasping the fillings with all other fingertips. Roll the bottom of the mat just over the fillings, tucking the fillings tightly under the fold. (Do not allow the mat to get stuck inside the roll!)

Lift the edge of the mat. Continue rolling until the roll is complete and the seam is facing down. Gently shape the roll by pressing your forefingers on top of the mat while simultaneously pressing your thumbs and middle fingers on the sides.

Allow the roll to rest seam-side down on a cutting board for at least 2 minutes. Repeat with remaining ingredients to make 3 more rolls.

Dip the blade of a very sharp knife in water. Use a swift sawing motion to cut each roll into 5 pieces. Serve with Ponzu Sauce for dipping.

# Summer Corn and Pickled Okra Rolls

My use of pickled okra has become somewhat of a "signature" throughout my sushi career. It is a nod to my Southern roots, and I almost always feature it in some form. Here, I like it paired with fresh corn kernels. If the corn is very sweet and fresh, you can forego blanching it.

**Rice Prep Time: Up to 1½ hours**
**Sushi Prep Time: 15 minutes**
**Makes 4 Rolls (20 pieces)**

Four 4 x 7-in (10 x 18-cm) nori sheets
3 cups (600 g) Traditional Sushi
   Rice, Brown Sushi Rice, Quinoa
   Sushi "Rice" or Multi-Grain Sushi
   Rice (pages 21-23)
2 teaspoons toasted sesame seeds
2 green onions (scallions), thinly
   sliced
8 large pickled okra
½ carrot, peeled and cut into
   matchsticks
½ red bell pepper, cut into
   matchsticks
4 tablespoons corn kernels, blanched

Place a 4 x 7-in (10 x 18-cm) sheet of nori vertically on a bamboo rolling mat. Make sure that the short end is parallel to the bottom of the mat and that the rough side is facing upwards.

Dip your fingertips lightly in cool water and spread about ¾ cup (150 g) of the sushi rice evenly over the bottom ¾ of the nori.

Sprinkle ½ teaspoon of the sesame seeds over the rice. Sprinkle ¼ of the green onions over the rice. Arrange 2 pieces of pickled okra end to end across the center of the sushi rice, making sure they extend to both edges of the nori. Lay ¼ of the carrots and red bell peppers in neat lines above the pickled okra. Add 1 tablespoon of the corn kernels in a neat line across the rice.

Wet your fingertips again and slide your thumbs underneath the mat while grasping the fillings with all other fingertips. Roll the bottom of the mat just over the fillings, tucking the fillings tightly under the fold. (Do not allow the mat to get stuck inside the roll!)

Lift the edge of the mat. Continue rolling until the roll is complete and the seam is facing down. Gently shape the roll by pressing your forefingers on top of the mat while simultaneously pressing your thumbs and middle fingers on the sides.

Allow the roll to rest seam-side down on a cutting board for at least 2 minutes. Repeat with remaining ingredients to make 3 more rolls.

To cut the rolls, dip the blade of a very sharp knife in water. Use a swift sawing motion to cut each roll into 5 pieces.

# Cucumber-Wrapped Rolls

In sushi school, one of the skills we worked on daily was learning to cut vegetables into long, thin continuous sheets that could be used as wrappers. It requires a special kind of knife as well as a special kind of patience. These cucumber-wrapped rolls offer a similar flavor without all of the headache by using a spoon to hollow out the cucumbers.

Rice Prep Time: Up to 1½ hours (note that Ponzu Sauce should be made a day in advance)
Sushi Prep Time: 20 minutes
Makes 4 Rolls (20 pieces)

Four 7-in (18-cm) lengths whole cucumber
1 cup (200 g) Traditional Sushi Rice, Brown Sushi Rice, Quinoa Sushi "Rice" or Multi-Grain Sushi Rice (pages 21–23)
2 mint sprigs, finely chopped
1 cup (250 g) Edamame Hummus (page 45) or store-bought hummus
One 4-in (10-cm) length carrot, cut into thin matchsticks
½ cup (85 g) pomegranate arils, or more, to taste
Vegetarian Ponzu Sauce (page 26)

Cut each cucumber length in half crosswise. Use a spoon to hollow out the core of each cucumber.

Mix the sushi rice with the chopped mint. Use a wet spoon to press 2 tablespoons of sushi rice into each cucumber, leaving room for the remaining ingredients.

Spoon the Edamame Hummus into a plastic bag. Snip away one corner of the bag and squeeze some hummus inside each cucumber piece. At this point, turning the cucumbers onto their sides rather than standing them on end will keep the filling from slipping out.

Slide some carrot sticks inside each cucumber. Use a chopstick or spoon to poke several pomegranate arils inside each cucumber. Seal with a dollop of the remaining Edamame Hummus.

Dip the blade of a very sharp knife in water. Use a swift sawing motion to cut each roll into 2 or 3 pieces. Sprinkle more pomegranate arils on top of each piece if desired. Serve with Ponzu Sauce for dipping.

Use a spoon to hollow out cucumbers.

Press rice into each cucumber.

Squeeze Edamame Hummus inside.

Insert pomegranate arils.

Slice the filled cucumbers.

# Sweet Potato and Shiitake Rolls

**I enjoy sweet potatoes in almost any form, especially when the flavor is sweet and salty. As an alternative to boiled sweet potatoes, try Soy Glazed Sweet Potatoes (page 44).**

Rice Prep Time: Up to 1½ hours
Sushi Prep Time: 30 minutes
Makes 4 rolls (20 pieces)

1½ cups (375 ml) water
1 cup (250 ml) soy sauce
4 tablespoons mirin or sherry
½ small sweet potato, peeled and
    cut into chopstick-width lengths
4 large shiitake mushrooms, wiped
    and stems removed
Four 4 x 7-in (10 x 18-cm) nori sheets
3 cups (600 g) Traditional Sushi
    Rice, Brown Sushi Rice, Quinoa
    Sushi "Rice" or Multi-Grain Sushi
    Rice (pages 21–23)
2 oz (60 g) daikon radish sprouts
    (*kaiware*) or pea sprouts
4 teaspoons slivered almonds, toasted

Bring the water, soy sauce and mirin to a boil in a saucepan. Add the sweet potato pieces and cook until soft, about 3–4 minutes. Remove and allow to cool and drain on paper towels, reserving the cooking liquid for mushrooms. Add mushrooms to the liquid. Reduce heat and simmer for 5 minutes. Remove mushrooms. Pat dry and allow them to cool, then slice them into thin strips.

Place a 4 x 7-in (10 x 18-cm) sheet of nori vertically on a bamboo rolling mat. Make sure that the short end is parallel to the bottom of the mat and that the rough side is facing upwards.

Dip your fingertips lightly in cool water and spread about ¾ cup (150 g) of the sushi rice evenly over the bottom ¾ of the nori. Arrange ¼ of the sweet potato pieces horizontally across the middle of the rice, making sure that they extend to both edges of the nori. Add ¼ of the mushroom pieces and daikon sprouts. Sprinkle 1 teaspoon of the almonds over the top.

Wet your fingers again and slide your thumbs underneath the mat while grasping the fillings with fingertips. Roll the bottom of the mat just over the fillings, tucking the fillings tightly under the fold. (Do not allow the mat to get stuck inside the roll!)

Lift the edge of the mat. Continue rolling until the roll is complete and the seam is facing down. Gently shape the roll by pressing your forefingers on top of the mat while simultaneously pressing your thumbs and middle fingers on the sides.

Allow the roll to rest seam-side down on a cutting board for at least 2 minutes. Repeat to make 3 more rolls.

To cut the rolls, dip the blade of a very sharp knife in water. Use a swift sawing motion to cut each roll into 5 pieces.

# Mushroom "Spider" Rolls

**Typically, spider sushi rolls feature a fried soft-shell crab inside a thick roll. The playful name describes how the legs of the crab extend beyond the sides of the roll. Here, fried *shimeji* and *enoki* mushrooms provide a similar, vegetarian-friendly effect.**

Rice Prep Time: Up to 1½ hours
Sushi Prep Time: 30 minutes
Makes 4 Rolls (20 pieces)

Oil for frying
Five 4 x 7-in (10 x 18-cm) nori sheets
One 4-oz (115-g) package shimeji
  mushrooms, wiped cleaned and trimmed
One 2-oz (60-g) package enoki
  mushrooms, wiped clean and trimmed
Potato starch or cornstarch (corn flour)
  for dusting

½ cup (125 ml) Vegan Tempura Batter
  (page 34)
3 cups (600 g) Traditional Sushi Rice,
  Brown Sushi Rice, Quinoa Sushi "Rice"
  or Multi-Grain Sushi Rice (pages 21–23)
4 tablespoons Faux Roe (page 68)
1 Japanese cucumber, deseeded and cut
  into matchsticks
2 oz (60 g) daikon radish, cut into
  matchsticks
2 romaine lettuce leaves, cut in half
  lengthwise

Heat 1 in (2.5 cm) of oil in a medium skillet over high heat. When the oil reaches 350°F (175°C), reduce the heat to maintain temperature as needed.

Cut 1 sheet of the nori into 4 strips. Divide the mushrooms into 4 equal piles, keeping the caps all in the same direction. For each mushroom "spider," turn the half the mushrooms in one pile around, then use a nori strip to bind the mushroom bundle in the center. Some caps should be facing outward on both ends. Repeat with remaining mushrooms and nori. Dust each mushroom "spider" with potato starch or corn starch. Shake away the excess before dipping into the tempura batter. Fry the mushroom "spiders" in oil until crisp. Drain on wire rack.

Place a 4 x 7-in (10 x 18-cm) sheet of nori vertically on a bamboo rolling mat. Make sure that the short end is parallel to the bottom of the mat and that the rough side is facing upwards. Dip your fingertips lightly in cool water and spread about ¾ cup (150 g) of the sushi rice evenly over the bottom ¾ of the nori.

Bind the mushroom bundles with a nori strip.

Fry and drain the tempura-dipped mushrooms.

Place nori vertically and top with rice and fillings.

Smear 1 teaspoon of the Faux Roe across the center of the sushi rice. Place one of the mushroom "spiders" on top and add ¼ of the cucumber and daikon radish. Top with a half lettuce leaf.

Wet your fingertips again and slide your thumbs underneath the mat while grasping the fillings with all other fingertips. Roll the bottom of the mat just over the fillings, tucking the fillings tightly under the fold. (Do not allow the mat to get stuck inside the roll!)

Lift the edge of the mat. Continue rolling until the roll is complete and the seam is facing down. Gently shape the roll by pressing your forefingers on top of the mat while simultaneously pressing your thumbs and middle fingers on the sides.

Allow the roll to rest seam-side down on a cutting board for at least 2 minutes. Repeat with remaining ingredients to make 3 more rolls. To cut the rolls, dip the blade of a very sharp knife in water. Use a swift sawing motion to cut each roll into 5 pieces. Arrange pieces on a serving tray or individual serving plates, prominently displaying the "spider" legs. Serve immediately.

# Coconut Tempura Tofu Rolls

**The tofu should be pressed so the batter will adhere to it. Place the block between two clean dishtowels or paper towels. Set a bowl holding a few canned items on top. Drain for 10 minutes.**

Rice Prep Time: Up to 1½ hours
Sushi Prep Time: 30 minutes
Makes 4 rolls (20 pieces)

Oil for frying
4 tablespoons unsweetened coconut flakes
4 tablespoons *panko* breadcrumbs
½ cup (125 ml) Vegan Tempura Batter (page 34)
4 oz (115 g) firm tofu, drained
Potato starch or cornstarch (corn flour) for dusting
Four 4 x 7-in (10 x 18-cm) nori sheets
3 cups (600 g) Traditional Sushi Rice or other sushi rice (pages 21-23)
2 oz (60 g) red cabbage, shredded
½ carrot, cut into thin matchsticks
1 green onion (scallion), thinly sliced
4 teaspoons chopped roasted peanuts
Curry Mayonnaise (page 29) for dipping

Heat 1 in (2.5 cm) of oil to 350°F (175°C) in a skillet over medium heat. Adjust heat as needed to maintain temperature.

Stir the coconut flakes and panko breadcrumbs into the tempura batter. Do not overmix.

Pat tofu dry and cut into chopstick-width lengths. Dust lightly with potato starch. Shake off excess, then dip into the coconut batter. Fry the tofu in the oil, turning as necessary until the coating is golden brown, about 2 minutes per side.

Drain on a wire rack.

Place a sheet of nori vertically on a bamboo rolling mat. Make sure the short end is parallel to the bottom of the mat and the rough side is facing upwards.

Dip your fingertips lightly in cool water and spread about ¾ cup (150 g) of the sushi rice evenly over the bottom ¾ of the nori.

Lay ¼ of the fried tofu horizontally across the center of the rice, making sure it extends to both edges of the nori. Then add ¼ of the cabbage, carrots and green onions. Sprinkle 1 teaspoon of peanuts over the top.

Wet your fingertips again and slide your thumbs underneath the mat while grasping the fillings with all other fingertips. Roll the bottom of the mat just over the fillings, tucking the fillings tightly under the fold. (Do not allow the mat to get stuck inside the roll!)

Lift the edge of the mat. Continue rolling until the roll is complete and the seam is facing down. Gently shape the roll by pressing your forefingers on top of the mat while simultaneously pressing your thumbs and middle fingers on the sides. Allow the roll to rest seam-side down on a cutting board for at least 2 minutes. Repeat with remaining ingredients to make 3 more rolls.

Dip the blade of a very sharp knife in water. Use a swift sawing motion to cut each roll into 5 pieces. Serve with Curry Mayonnaise for dipping.

# Chapter 6

# INSIDE-OUT ROLLS

It's easy to understand why sushi bar menus offer so many selections that feature the rice on the outside of the roll. Among the sushi varieties, inside-out rolls offer great versatility in fillings. Preparing inside-out rolls is one of the easier methods. It also allows you to really get to know your sushi, as the bamboo rolling mat is used just for shaping. Even rolls that are draped with colorful toppings only look complicated to prepare. The technique for wrapping a sushi roll in avocado (or strawberries) can be reproduced by anyone in a home kitchen.

If you've always wanted to try some of sushi's most popular and colorful rolls, inside-out rolls are a great beginning. California Rolls, "Dynamite" Tofu Rolls and Caterpillar Rolls are delicious vegetarian takes on mainstream rolls that could not otherwise be enjoyed due to their seafood fillings, sauces or toppings. Eggplant, Mushroom and Red Pepper Rolls; Honeydew Melon and Cucumber Dragon Rolls; and Sesame Strawberry Rhubarb Rolls are creations that boast compelling new flavor combinations.

# HOW TO MAKE INSIDE-OUT SUSHI ROLLS

1) Cover a bamboo rolling mat tightly with plastic wrap and set aside for later. This roll is constructed by rolling with your hands.

2) Begin with a 4 x 7-in (10 x 18-cm) piece of nori. Place the nori directly on your cutting board, making sure the long end is parallel to the bottom of the board and that the rough side is facing upwards.

3) Wet your fingertips lightly in cool water and spread about ¾ cup (150 g) of prepared sushi rice evenly over the entire surface of the nori.

4) Flip the nori over so that the rice is face down on the cutting board. Add the desired ingredients horizontally in the middle of the nori, making sure that the ingredients are distributed evenly and extend to both edges of the nori. For best results, use at least 2, but no more than 5, substantial fillings.

5) Wet your fingertips again and slide your thumbs underneath the nori while grasping fillings with all other fingertips. Roll the bottom of the nori just over the fillings, making sure to tightly tuck the fillings under the fold.

6) Continue rolling and tucking until the roll is completed. Use the bamboo rolling mat covered in plastic wrap to gently shape the roll. Press your forefingers on top of the mat while simultaneously pressing your thumbs and middle fingers into the sides.

7) Place the roll seam-side down on the cutting board. Dip the tip of a very sharp knife in water, and allow the water to run down the blade, then cut the roll into 8 pieces using a swift sawing motion.

## Tip
If using a wooden cutting board, wipe it down with damp cloth to prevent the rice from sticking.

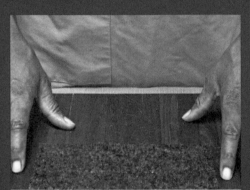
Place **nori** horizontally with the rough side up.

Cover the entire nori surface with sushi rice.

Flip **nori** over and add fillings across the center.

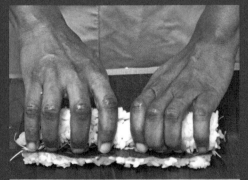
**Roll nori just over fillings, tuck and continue.**

**Shape completed roll with plastic-lined mat.**

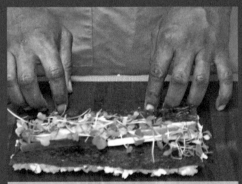
**Cut roll into 8 pieces.**

# California Rolls

The buttery feel of avocado across the palate inspired sushi chefs in the '70s, when an ingredient with a similar texture was nearly impossible to obtain in California. California Rolls get their name from the avocados they contain—the fruits grow abundantly there.

**Rice Prep Time: Up to 1½ hours**
**Sushi Prep Time: 15 minutes**
**Makes 4 rolls (32 pieces)**

**Four 4 x 7-in (10 x 18-cm) nori sheets**
**3 cups (600 g) Traditional Sushi Rice or Brown Sushi Rice (pages 21 and 23)**
**½ avocado, cut into 8 slices**
**1 English or Japanese cucumber, deseeded and cut into matchsticks**
**2 oz (60 g) daikon sprouts (*kaiware*) or pea sprouts**
**4 tablespoons Faux Roe (page 68)**

Place the nori directly on your cutting board, making sure that the long end is parallel to the bottom of the board and the rough side is facing upwards.

Wet your fingertips lightly in cool water and spread about ¾ cup (150 g) of sushi rice evenly over the entire surface of the nori.

Flip the nori over so that the rice is face down on the cutting board. Top with 2 avocado slices, making sure they extend to both edges of the nori. Add ¼ of the cucumber and daikon sprouts. Wet your fingertips again and slide your thumbs underneath the nori while grasping fillings with all other fingertips. Roll the bottom of the nori just over the fillings, making sure

to tightly tuck the fillings under the fold.

Continue rolling and tucking until the roll is completed. Use the bamboo rolling mat covered in plastic wrap to gently shape the roll, pressing forefingers on top of the mat while simultaneously pressing your thumbs and middle fingers into the sides.

Place the roll seam-side down on the cutting board. Dip the tip of a very sharp knife in water and allow the water to run down the blade. Cut the roll into 8 pieces using a swift sawing motion. Spread 1 tablespoon of the Faux Roe across the top of the cut pieces. Repeat with the remaining ingredients to make 3 more rolls.

# Roasted Poblano and Avocado Rolls

**This is a Tex-Mex-style sushi roll. Be sure to use cooked black beans, not Chinese black fermented soybeans. Kick up the South of the Border flavor by serving salsa alongside the rolls.**

**Rice Prep Time: Up to 1½ hours (note that the Ponzu Sauce must be made a day ahead)**
**Sushi Prep Time: 15 minutes**
**Makes 4 rolls (32 pieces)**

**Four 4 x 7-in (10 x 18-cm) nori sheets**
**3 cups (600 g) Traditional Sushi Rice or Brown Sushi Rice (pages 21 and 23)**
**½ cup (80 g) tortilla chips, finely crushed**
**½ avocado, cut into 8 wedges**
**1 roasted poblano pepper, peeled, deseeded and cut into thin strips**
**½ red bell pepper, cut into matchsticks**
**4 tablespoons cooked black beans, drained and roughly smashed**
**Vegetarian Ponzu Sauce (page 27), if desired**

Place the nori directly on your cutting board, making sure that the long end is parallel to the bottom of the board and the rough side faces up.

Wet your fingertips lightly in cool water and spread about ¾ cup (150 g) of sushi rice evenly over the entire surface of the nori. Sprinkle ¼ of the crushed tortilla chips over the rice and press gently.

Flip the nori over so that the rice is face down on the cutting board. Lay 2 avocado wedges across the center of the rice. Top with ¼ of the poblano slices and red bell pepper sticks. Sprinkle 1 tablespoon of the black beans on the top.

Wet your fingertips again and slide your thumbs underneath the nori while grasping fillings with all other fingertips. Roll the bottom of the nori just over the fillings, making sure to tuck the fillings under the fold tightly.

Continue rolling and tucking until the roll is

completed. Use the bamboo rolling mat covered in plastic wrap to gently shape the roll, pressing forefingers on top of the mat while simultaneously pressing your thumbs and middle fingers into the sides.

Place the roll seam-side down on the cutting board. Repeat steps to create 3 more rolls. Dip the tip of a very sharp knife in water and allow the water to run down the blade. Cut each roll into 8 pieces using a swift sawing motion. Serve with Ponzu Sauce, if desired.

# Tofu and Avocado Caterpillar Rolls

**Simmered tofu packets (inari) have a sweet and savory flavor that makes them a favorite when stuffed with tangy sushi rice. They're just as tasty cut into strips and tucked inside sushi rolls. Always pat away any excess liquid from the strips before adding them to sushi rolls so that the extra moisture doesn't unseal the rolls.**

1 avocado, sliced very thinly
Two 4 x 7-in (10 x 18-cm) nori sheets
1½ cups (300 g) prepared
  Traditional Sushi Rice or Brown
  Sushi Rice (pages 21 and 23)
4 inari pouches, cut into thin strips
½ English or Japanese cucumber,
  deseeded and cut into
  matchsticks
One 4-in (10-cm) length carrot,
  cut into matchsticks
2 tablespoons Vegetarian Eel
  Sauce (page 26)
1 teaspoon toasted sesame seeds

Rice Prep Time: Up to 1½ hours
Sushi Prep Time: 15 minutes
Makes 2 rolls (16 pieces)

Lay one sheet of nori on your cutting board and cover with a length of plastic film. Arrange half of the avocado strips on the plastic in a line across the center of the nori. (The slices should form backwards Cs, overlapping slightly.) Set the avocado sheet aside. Repeat with a second piece of film and the remaining avocado.

To assemble the rolls, place one nori sheet directly on your cutting board, making sure that the long end is parallel to the bottom of the board and the rough side is facing upwards.

Wet your fingertips lightly in cool water and spread about ¾ cup (150 g) of sushi rice evenly over the entire surface of the nori.

Flip the nori over so that the rice is face down on the cutting board. Lay ½ of the inari strips across the center of the nori. Top with ½ of the cucumber and carrot pieces.

Wet your fingertips again and slide your thumbs underneath the nori while grasping fillings with all other fingertips. Roll the bottom of the nori just over the fillings, making sure to tightly tuck the fillings under the fold.

Continue rolling and tucking until the roll is completed. With the bamboo rolling mat covered in plastic wrap, gently shape the roll by pressing forefingers on top of the mat while simultaneously pressing your thumbs and middle fingers into the sides.

Place the roll seam-side down on the cutting board. (Do not cut yet!) Make another roll with the remaining ingredients.

Invert one avocado sheet on top of the first sushi roll. Leaving the plastic wrap in place, use the bamboo rolling mat to press the avocado onto the roll. Repeat with the second roll and the other avocado sheet. Do not remove the plastic.

Dip the tip of a very sharp knife in water. Slice through the plastic wrap and cut each roll into 8 pieces. Use the bamboo rolling mat to press the avocado into the roll once more before removing the plastic wrap from each piece.

Arrange the pieces on a serving tray. Drizzle with the Vegetarian Eel Sauce and sprinkle with the sesame seeds.

# Honeydew Melon and Cucumber Dragon Rolls

How can you distinguish the difference between caterpillar sushi rolls and dragon rolls? Both are beautiful rolls draped gracefully in vibrant avocado. Caterpillar sushi rolls typically include mild fillings and are served with a sweet sauce. Dragon sushi rolls, on the other hand, boast a fiery filling. Like these crisp, fresh rolls, they are often served with a bold and spicy sauce.

Rice Prep Time: Up to 1½ hours
Sushi Prep Time: 15 minutes
Makes 2 rolls (16 pieces)

1 avocado, sliced very thinly
Two 4 x 7-in (10 x 18-cm) nori sheets
1½ cups (300 g) Traditional Sushi Rice or Brown Sushi Rice (pages 21 and 23)
2 teaspoons fresh coriander leaves (cilantro), finely minced
8 oz (225 g) honeydew melon, cut into 4-in (10-cm) lengths
1 jalapeno pepper, deseeded and cut into thin matchsticks
One 4-in (10-cm) length English or Japanese cucumber, deseeded and cut into matchsticks
Dragon Juice Sauce, to taste

Lay one sheet of nori on your cutting board and cover with a length of plastic film. Arrange half of the avocado slices on the plastic in a line across the center of the nori. (Slices should form backwards Cs, overlapping slightly.) Set aside; repeat with the remaining avocado slices and a second piece of film.

Place one nori sheet directly on your cutting board, making sure that the long end is parallel to the bottom of the board and the rough side is facing upwards.

Wet your fingertips lightly. Spread about ¾ cup (150 g) of sushi rice evenly over the entire surface of the nori.

Flip the nori over so that the rice is face down on the cutting board. Spread 1 teaspoon of the fresh coriander leaves across the center of the nori. Top with ½ of the honeydew melon, jalapeno and cucumber, making sure that the fillings are spread evenly and extend to both edges of the nori.

Wet your fingertips again and slide your thumbs underneath the nori while grasping fillings with all other fingertips. Roll the bottom of the nori just over the fillings, making sure to tightly tuck the fillings under the fold.

Continue rolling and tucking until the roll is completed. Use the bamboo rolling mat covered in plastic wrap to gently shape the roll, pressing forefingers on top of the mat while simultaneously pressing your thumbs and middle fingers into the sides.

Place the roll seam side-down on the cutting board. (Do not cut yet!) Repeat steps to make another roll.

Invert one avocado sheet on top of the first sushi roll. Leaving the plastic wrap in place, use the bamboo rolling mat to press the avocado onto the roll. Repeat with the second roll and the other avocado sheet.

Wet the tip of a very sharp knife. Slice through the plastic wrap and cut each roll into 8 pieces. Use the bamboo mat to press the avocado into the roll once more before removing the plastic. Arrange the pieces on a serving tray. Drizzle with Dragon Juice Sauce, to taste.

# Dragon Juice Sauce

Prep Time: 5 minutes
Makes 1 cup (250 ml)

½ cup (100 g) *umeboshi* (pickled plum) paste
½ cup (125 ml) water
1 jalapeno pepper, deseeded and chopped
2 tablespoons grated fresh ginger

Place all ingredients in a blender. Pulse once or twice, then blend the mixture for 30 seconds. Check to see whether the sauce is smooth. If small bits remain, blend again for 30 seconds. Chill the sauce until ready for use.

Cover the entire nori surface with sushi rice.

Flip and place cucumber and melons in the center.

Roll edge of nori over fillings, and complete roll.

Invert avocado-covered sheet over roll and press.

Cut roll into 8 pieces with plastic wrap intact.

Remove plastic wrap before serving.

# Mango, Avocado and Kimchi Rolls

**Spicy kimchi is tempered with creamy avocado, while the mango adds sweetness. If you prefer a less sweet flavor, try using green papaya instead. Be sure to squeeze the kimchi before using it—if the roll is too wet, it will not seal properly and will fall apart when you cut it.**

Four 4 x 7-in (10 x 18-cm) nori sheets
3 cups (600 g) Traditional Sushi Rice or Brown Sushi Rice (pages 21 and 23)
4 teaspoons toasted sesame seeds
½ avocado, cut into 8 slices
½ cup (100 g) store-bought kimchi or Vegan Kimchi (page 49), drained well and patted dry
½ mango, cut into thin strips
4 tablespoons Faux Roe (page 68)

**Rice Prep Time: Up to 1½ hours**
**Sushi Prep Time: 15 minutes**
**Makes 4 rolls (32 pieces)**

Place a sheet of nori directly on your cutting board, making sure that the long end is parallel to the bottom of the board and the rough side faces up.

Wet your fingertips lightly in cool water and spread about ¾ cup (150 g) of sushi rice evenly over the entire surface of the nori. Sprinkle 1 teaspoon of the sesame seeds over the rice.

Flip the nori over so that the rice is face down on the cutting board. Place 2 avocado slices horizontally in the middle of the nori. Add ¼ of the kimchi and ¼ of the mango, making sure that the fillings are distributed evenly and extend to both edges of the nori.

Wet your fingertips again and slide your thumbs underneath the nori while grasping fillings with all other fingertips. Roll the bottom of the nori just over the fillings, making sure to tuck the fillings tightly under the fold.

Continue rolling and tucking until the roll is completed. Use the bamboo rolling mat covered in plastic wrap to gently shape the roll, pressing forefingers on top of the mat while simultaneously pressing your thumbs and middle fingers into the sides.

Place the roll seam-side down on the cutting board. Repeat the previous steps to make 3 more rolls. Smear 1 tablespoon of Faux Roe across the top of each sushi roll. Dip the tip of a very sharp knife in water and allow the water to run down the blade. Cut each roll into 8 pieces using a swift sawing motion.

# Eggplant, Mushroom and Red Bell Pepper Rolls

**Store-bought roasted red bell peppers can often have a briny taste. If you prefer a more neutral flavor, try roasting your own bell peppers. Generously oil a red bell pepper, then place it on a baking sheet. Roast it in the oven at 350°F (175°C) until the skin begins to turn black. Once it is cool, peel and deseed the pepper.**

Rice Prep Time: Up to 1½ hours
Sushi Prep Time: 15 minutes
Makes 4 rolls (32 pieces)

1 Japanese eggplant or ½ small globe eggplant, cut into 4-in (10-cm) lengths
1 teaspoon dark sesame oil
2 teaspoons soy sauce
Four 4 x 7-in (10 x 18-cm) nori sheets
3 cups (600 g) Traditional Sushi Rice or Brown Sushi Rice (pages 21 and 23)
8 shiitake mushrooms, thinly sliced
1 roasted red pepper, deseeded, patted dry, and sliced into strips
1 green onion (scallion), thinly sliced

Heat an oven to 350°F (175°C). Lightly grease a baking sheet. Toss the eggplant pieces with dark sesame oil and soy sauce. Roast eggplant for 8–10 minutes. Cool completely before using.

Place the nori directly on your cutting board, making sure the long end is parallel to the bottom of the board and that the rough side is facing upwards.

Wet your fingertips lightly in cool water and spread about ¾ cup (150 g) of sushi rice evenly over the entire surface of the nori.

Flip the nori over so that the rice is face down on the cutting board. Arrange ¼ of the eggplant pieces across the center of the nori. Top with ¼ of the shiitake slices.

Wet your fingertips again and slide your thumbs underneath the nori while grasping fillings with all other fingertips. Roll the bottom of the nori just over the fillings, making sure to tightly tuck the fillings under the fold.

Continue rolling and tucking until the roll is completed. With the bamboo rolling mat covered in plastic wrap, gently shape the roll by pressing forefingers on top of the mat while simultaneously pressing your thumbs and middle fingers into the sides.

Place the roll seam-side down on the cutting board. Repeat with remaining ingredients for 3 more rolls. (Do not cut yet!)

Lay the roasted pepper strips across the top of each roll. Lay a sheet of plastic wrap on top of each roll. Dip the tip of a very sharp knife in water, and cut each roll into 8 pieces. Use the bamboo rolling mat to shape and press the roasted red pepper strips into each roll once more before removing plastic wrap.

Arrange pieces on a serving dish and garnish with green onion slices.

# Sesame Strawberry Rhubarb Rolls

**Strawberries for sushi? Why not! Thin slices of the fruit lie elegantly on top of a roll filled with sesame rhubarb. Use a mandoline to slice the strawberries as thinly as possible. Be sure to blot the strawberries dry with a clean dishtowel or paper towel before placing them on the sushi roll, or they will not adhere easily.**

Rice Prep Time: Up to 1½ hours
Sushi Prep Time: 15 minutes
Makes 2 rolls (16 pieces)

1 cup (200 g) sugar
2 cups (500 ml) water
Four 4-in (10-cm) stalks rhubarb
4 tablespoons soy sauce
8 large strawberries, sliced very thinly
Two 4 x 7-in (10 x 18-cm) nori sheets
1½ cups (300 g) Traditional Sushi Rice or Brown Sushi Rice (pages 21 and 23)
4 inari pouches, cut into thin strips
1 oz (30 g) daikon radish, shredded
2 tablespoons Vegetarian Eel Sauce (page 26)
1 teaspoon toasted sesame seeds

In a medium pan over high heat, dissolve the sugar in the water. Add the rhubarb and soy sauce. Boil for 10 minutes, or until the rhubarb is tender but still holds its shape. Remove rhubarb from liquid and allow to cool.

Lay one sheet of nori on your cutting board and cover with a length of plastic film. Arrange half the strawberry slices in two overlapping lines across the center of the nori. Set the strawberry sheet aside and repeat with a second piece of plastic wrap.

To assemble the rolls, place one sheet of nori directly on your cutting board, making sure that the long end is parallel to the bottom of the board and the rough side is facing upwards.

Wet your fingertips lightly and spread about ¾ cup (150 g) of sushi rice evenly over the entire surface of the nori.

Flip the nori over so that the rice is face down on the cutting board. Add half of the inari strips across the center of the nori. Top with half of the rhubarb and daikon pieces.

Wet your fingertips again and slide your thumbs underneath the nori while grasping fillings with all other fingertips. Roll the bottom of the nori just over the fillings, making sure to tightly tuck the fillings under the fold.

Continue rolling and tucking until the roll is completed. Use the bamboo rolling mat covered in plastic wrap to gently shape the roll, pressing forefingers on top of the mat while simultaneously pressing your thumbs and middle fingers into the sides.

Place the roll seam-side down on the cutting board. (Do not cut yet!) Make another roll with the remaining ingredients.

Invert one strawberry sheet over the first sushi roll. Leave the plastic wrap in place and press the strawberries onto the roll with the bamboo mat. Repeat with the second roll.

Wet the tip of a very sharp knife. Leaving the plastic wrap in place, slice each roll into 8 pieces. Use the mat to press the strawberries into the roll again before removing plastic wrap. Arrange the pieces on a serving tray. Drizzle with Vegetarian Eel Sauce and sprinkle with sesame seeds.

# Peanut Carrot Rolls

**Peanuts make an excellent substitute for crunchy tempura flakes. They have a similar appearance and provide just the right amount of crunch. The best part? Unlike tempura flakes, there is nothing to fry. For best results, use lightly salted roasted peanuts. Be sure to chop the peanuts by hand, as using a food processor can result in peanut paste.**

Rice Prep Time: Up to 1½ hours
Sushi Prep Time: 15 minutes
Makes 4 rolls (32 pieces)

1 carrot, peeled and cut into matchsticks
3 tablespoons Sushi Rice Dressing (page 20)
Four 4 x 7-in (10 x 18-cm) nori sheets
3 cups (600 g) Traditional Sushi Rice or Brown Sushi Rice (pages 21 and 23)
4 tablespoons roasted peanuts, finely chopped
8 shiitake mushrooms, thinly sliced
8 snow peas, sliced in half lengthwise
1 celery stalk, cut into matchsticks
2 oz (60 g) daikon sprouts (*kaiware*) or pea sprouts
4 tablespoons Black Bean Sauce (page 25), or more, to taste

Toss the carrot matchsticks with the Sushi Rice Dressing and set aside.

Place one nori sheet directly on the cutting board, making sure the long end is parallel to the bottom of the board and that the rough side is facing upwards.

Wet your fingertips lightly in cool water and spread about ¾ cup (150 g) of sushi rice evenly over the entire surface of the nori. Spread 1 tablespoon of roasted peanuts over the rice. Press peanuts into the rice.

Flip the nori over so that the rice is face down on the cutting board. Drain the carrots and squeeze out any excess liquid. Lay ¼ of the carrots across the center of the nori. Top with ¼ of the shiitake mushrooms, snow peas, celery and daikon sprouts.

Wet your fingertips again and slide your thumbs underneath the nori while grasping fillings with all other fingertips. Roll the bottom of the nori just over the fillings, making sure to tightly tuck the fillings under the fold.

Continue rolling and tucking until the roll is completed. With the bamboo rolling mat covered in plastic wrap, gently shape the roll by pressing forefingers on top of the mat while simultaneously pressing your thumbs and middle fingers into the sides.

Place the roll seam-side down on the cutting board. Repeat with remaining nori and fillings to make 3 more rolls.

To serve the rolls, dip the tip of a very sharp knife in water and cut each roll into 8 pieces using a swift sawing motion. Arrange pieces on a serving dish. Drizzle with Black Bean Sauce.

# Kaleidoscope Rice Paper Rolls

**I hope you will humor me. Instead of having sushi rice on the outside, they are wrapped in rice paper for an alternative type of inside-out roll. A bit of fresh beet is used to tint the sushi rice pink, but a rainbow of other colors can be achieved with a drop or two of food coloring.**

**Rice Prep Time: Up to 1½ hours**
**Sushi Prep Time: 30 minutes**
**Makes 2 rolls (10 pieces)**

**Four 8½ x 8½-in (20 x 20-cm)**
  **sheets rice paper**
**3 cups (600 g) Traditional**
  **Sushi Rice or Brown Sushi**
  **Rice (pages 21 and 23)**
**1 teaspoon finely grated beet**
**2 Japanese cucumbers, cut into**
  **quarters lengthwise**
**Two 4 x 7-in (10 x 18-cm)**
  **nori sheets**
**8 matchstick-width strips**
  **mango**

Stack 2 sheets of rice paper and run under warm water for about 1 minute. The rice paper should begin to soften and become pliable. Pat away excess water before folding the stacked sheets in half lengthwise

Place half the sushi rice in a small bowl and toss with the grated beet. Continue tossing until mixture becomes evenly pink. Set aside.

Place the folded rice paper vertically on your cutting board. Wet your fingertips lightly in cool water and spread half of the beet-tinted sushi rice evenly over the bottom half of the rice paper.

Arrange two of the cucumber quarters on the pink rice. Each cucumber quarter should lie at the outermost bottom and top edges of the rice. The green skins should face outward. Set aside.

Place one sheet of nori on a bamboo rolling mat, making sure the short end is parallel to the bottom of the board and that the rough side is facing upwards. Spread half of the un-tinted sushi rice evenly across the bottom half of the nori. Wet your fingertips again and slide your thumbs underneath the mat. Begin rolling the bottom of the mat just over the edge of the nori. Lift the edge of the mat and continue rolling the rice and nori to form a tight log.

Transfer the rice paper to a bamboo rolling mat. Nestle the nori and rice log snugly in the center of the beet-tinted rice. Place two strips of mango on top of each cucumber quarter. Place another cucumber wedge on top of each of the cucumber wedges. Again, the outer green skins should face outward.

Wet your fingertips and slide your thumbs underneath the rice paper while grasping fillings with all other fingertips. Roll the bottom of the rice paper just over the fillings, making sure to tightly tuck the fillings under the fold.

Continue rolling and tucking until the roll is completed. Use the bamboo mat to gently shape the roll by pressing forefingers on top of the mat while simultaneously pressing your thumbs and middle fingers into the sides.

Place the roll seam-side down on the cutting board. Repeat steps with the remaining ingredients to make a second roll. Dip the tip of a very sharp knife in water and allow the water to run down the blade. Cut each roll into 5 pieces using a swift sawing motion.

Fold softened rice paper in half and stack.

Toss beets with rice until mixture is pink.

Create first layer of rice and cucumber.

Spread un-tinted rice on nori and roll.

Add mango strips and more cucumbers.

Roll rice paper over all fillings.

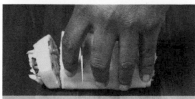
Cut roll into 5 pieces.

# "Dynamite" Tofu Rolls

Dynamite rolls, also referred to as volcano rolls, are rolls that appear to explode over the top with a broiled seafood and mayonnaise topping. Here, tofu shirataki noodles duplicate the texture of the crab that is often used. For extra flavor, try adding Basic Furikake Seasoning.

Rice Prep Time: Up to 1½ hours
Sushi Prep Time: 15 minutes
Makes 4 rolls (32 pieces)

4 California Rolls (page 95), cut into pieces, Faux Roe (page 68) reserved on the side
8 oz (250 g) tofu *shirataki* angel hair noodles, drained
1 cup (250 ml) Curry Mayonnaise (page 29)
1 green onion (scallion), thinly sliced
2 teaspoons sesame seeds, toasted

Cut the shirataki into strings about 4 inches (10 cm) long. Place in a bowl and mix with the Curry Mayonnaise and Faux Roe.

Turn broiler on high. Place the shirataki mixture on a sheet of aluminum foil and broil for 2 minutes or until the mayonnaise is bubbly.

Arrange each California Roll onto a serving platter. Slide some of the warm shirataki mixture over each piece. Top with green onions and sesame seeds.

# Chapter 7

# HAND ROLLS

Hand rolls are sushi simplicity itself: Roll. Eat. Repeat.

As the name implies, hand rolls are prepared in your hand. Place nori on your palm, layer it with rice and toppings, and then roll it into a loose cone. No bamboo rolling mat is need to confine them into a tight roll. No knife is used to cut them into bite-sized pieces.

The only difficulty of hand rolls can be figuring out how to eat them. Does the first bite come from the top or the bottom? Should the sauce be poured into the cone or should the cone be dipped into the sauce? Starting at either end should not present a dilemma on a properly formed hand roll, as they will both have sufficient proportions of rice and fillings. Pouring sauce into the cone can cause a mess, as the sauce will flow through the bottom and perhaps take valuable fillings with it. Dipping produces yet another problem: the fillings tend to flop over into the sauce. Try tilting your hand roll to the side and adding a bit of sauce as you eat the roll. Ultimately, the choice of how to eat a hand roll is yours. The only real rule is to consume it shortly after preparation, while the nori is still crispy.

If you are left-handed, begin with the nori in your right palm. Transpose the instructions on the following page to adjust for rolling in the right hand.

# HOW TO MAKE SUSHI HAND ROLLS

**1)** Align the nori horizontally in your left palm, making sure that the rough side of the nori faces up. Dip a wooden spoon or plastic measuring spoon into water before using it to apply 4 teaspoons of prepared sushi rice vertically on the nori. Cover about a third of the surface from the left side.

**2)** Place your chosen fillings vertically down the center of the rice. Take the bottom left corner of the nori and fold it over the ingredients until it reaches the top point just beyond the rice. (Don't pull too tight or the nori will snap!)

**3)** Roll the nori downward, forming a tight cone. Secure the loose edge with a single grain of rice. Eat immediately.

Spread rice across ⅓ of the nori, starting at left.

Add desired fillings.

Roll the nori to form a tight cone.

# Daikon and Kimchi Hand Rolls

**I really enjoy kimchi with tangy sushi rice. You can use much more kimchi in a hand roll than in other types of sushi rolls. For an interesting twist, try this roll with pickled daikon (*takuan*).**

**Rice Prep Time: Up to 1½ hours**
**Sushi Prep Time: 10 minutes**
**Makes 4 rolls**

Four 4 x 7-in (10 x 18-cm) nori sheets
1 cup (200 g) Traditional Sushi Rice, Brown Sushi Rice, Quinoa Sushi
  "Rice" or Multi-Grain Sushi Rice (pages 21–23)
8 strips daikon radish, about the size of french fries
1 cup (200 g) store-bought kimchi or Vegan Kimchi (page 49)
½ tomato, cut into 8 wedges
Daikon sprouts (*kaiware*) or pea sprouts, to taste (optional)

Align 1 sheet of nori across your left palm with the rough side facing up. Press 4 tablespoons of the sushi rice on the leftmost third of the nori.

Arrange 2 daikon radish strips in a line down the center of the rice. Add ¼ of the kimchi. Top with 2 wedges of tomato. Add daikon sprouts, if desired.

Take the bottom left corner of the nori and fold it over the fillings until it reaches the top point just beyond the rice. Roll downward, forming a tight cone, until all the nori has been wrapped around. If desired, secure the loose edge with a single grain of rice.

Repeat steps with the remaining nori, rice and fillings to make 3 more rolls. Serve immediately.

# Pickled Green Tomato Hand Rolls

Curry is another one of those unexpected flavors that I like to include in sushi. The flavor pairs especially well with cauliflower and fresh coriander leaves (cilantro). Pickled green tomatoes are a crisp treat. If you can't find them at your local supermarket, try your local farmers' market.

**Rice Prep Time: Up to 1½ hours**
**Sushi Prep Time: 10 minutes**
**Makes 4 rolls**

Four 4 x 7-in (10 x 18-cm) nori sheets

1 cup (200 g) Traditional Sushi Rice, Brown Sushi Rice, Quinoa Sushi "Rice" or Multi-Grain Sushi Rice (pages 21–23)

4 teaspoons Curry Mayonnaise (page 29)

4 teaspoons Curry Furikake (page 30)

4 sprigs fresh coriander leaves (cilantro), or more, to taste

One 4-in (10-cm) length cucumber, deseeded and cut into matchsticks

8 pickled green tomatoes, drained

4 cauliflower florets, steamed and cut in half lengthwise

Align 1 sheet of nori across your left palm with the rough side facing up. Press 4 tablespoons of the sushi rice on the leftmost third of the nori.

Spread 1 teaspoon of Curry Mayonnaise down the rice and sprinkle with 1 teaspoon Curry Furikake. Place one or more sprigs fresh coriander on the rice. Add ¼ of the cucumbers and top with 2 pieces of pickled green tomato and 2 cauliflower pieces.

Take the bottom left corner of the nori and fold it over the fillings until it reaches the top point just beyond the rice. Roll downward, forming a tight cone, until all the nori has been wrapped around. If desired, secure the loose edge with a single grain of rice.

Repeat steps with the remaining ingredients to make 3 more rolls. Serve immediately.

# Pickled Radish Hand Rolls

**If you can't locate _takuan_ (pickled daikon), substitute some well-drained Daikon Slaw (page 55). The flavor is different, but it still pairs quite well with the sweet, tart pickled plum paste.**

**Rice Prep Time: Up to 1½ hours**
**Sushi Prep Time: 10 minutes**
**Makes 4 rolls**

Four 4 x 7-in (10 x 18-cm) nori sheets

1 cup (200 g) prepared Traditional
  Sushi Rice or other sushi rice
  (pages 21–23)

4 teaspoons _umeboshi_ (pickled plum)
  paste

8 large shiso (perilla) or basil leaves

2 inari pouches, cut into thin strips

8 strips _takuan_ (pickled daikon),
  about the size of french fries

Align 1 sheet of nori across your left palm with the rough side facing up. Press 4 tablespoons of the sushi rice on the left third of the nori.

Spread 1 teaspoon of umeboshi paste down the rice. Arrange 2 large shiso or basil leaves down the center of the rice. Add ¼ of the inari strips and top with 2 pieces of takuan.

Take the bottom left corner of the nori and fold it over the fillings until it reaches the top point just beyond the rice. Roll downward, forming a tight cone, until all the nori has been wrapped around. Secure the loose edge with a single grain of rice.

Repeat steps to make 3 more rolls. Serve immediately.

# Vegetarian BLT Rolls

Cook the vegan bacon just before assembling this roll. The warmth of the bacon with the crisp, cool romaine lettuce offers a pleasant overall experience. Adding Vegetarian Eel Sauce eliminates the need for soy sauce.

Rice Prep Time: Up to 1½ hours
Sushi Prep Time: 10 minutes
Makes 4 rolls

Four 4 x 7-in (10 x 18-cm) nori sheets
1 cup (200 g) Traditional Sushi Rice, Brown Sushi Rice, Quinoa Sushi "Rice" or Multi-Grain Sushi Rice (pages 21–23)
8 strips vegan bacon
1 romaine lettuce leaf, cut into thin strips
¼ avocado, cut into 4 wedges
½ tomato, cut into 8 wedges
4 tablespoons Vegetarian Eel Sauce (page 26), or more, to taste
4 teaspoons toasted sesame seeds

Cook the vegan bacon according to package instructions.

Align a sheet of nori across your left palm with the rough side facing up. Press 4 tablespoons of the sushi rice on the left third of the nori.

Arrange 2 strips of the vegan bacon down the center of the rice. Top with ¼ of the romaine lettuce, then add 1 avocado wedge and 2 tomato wedges. Drizzle 1 tablespoon of Vegetarian Eel Sauce over the fillings and sprinkle with 1 teaspoon of the sesame seeds.

Take the bottom left corner of the nori and fold it over the fillings until it reaches the top point just beyond the rice. Roll downward, forming a tight cone, until all the nori has been wrapped around. If desired, secure the loose edge with a single grain of rice.

Repeat steps with the remaining ingredients to make 3 more rolls. Serve immediately.

# Soba Hand Rolls

If you're gluten free, be sure to check the ingredients list on your soba (buckwheat) noodles. Some contain a mix of grains, including wheat. Price is often a reflection: soba made with 100% buckwheat often costs more than noodles made with wheat mixed in.

**Rice Prep Time: Up to 1½ hours**
**Sushi Prep Time: 10 minutes**
**Makes 4 rolls**

3 oz (90 g) dry soba (buckwheat) noodles
4 tablespoons Sesame Dressing (page 28)
4 teaspoons Basic Furikake Seasoning (page 30)
Four 4 x 7-in (10 x 18-cm) nori sheets
1 green onion (scallion), thinly sliced
½ carrot, shredded
8 snow peas, cut into thin strips
Daikon sprouts (*kaiware*) or pea sprouts, to taste

Bring a large pot of unsalted water to a boil over high heat. Add the soba noodles and stir. Boil for about 7 minutes. Test a noodle—it should be cooked through but not mushy. Drain and rinse the noodles under cold water. Transfer to a bowl and toss with the Sesame Dressing and Basic Furikake Seasoning.

Align 1 sheet of nori across your left palm with the rough side facing up. Lay ¼ of the buckwheat noodle mixture on the left third of the nori.

Sprinkle with ¼ of the green onions and add ¼ of the carrots and snow peas. Add daikon sprouts, to taste.

Take the bottom left corner of the nori and fold it over the fillings until it reaches the top point just beyond the noodles. Roll downward, forming a tight cone, until all the nori has been wrapped around.

Repeat steps with the remaining ingredients to make 3 more rolls. Serve immediately.

# Japanese Omelette Hand Rolls

Don't be fooled by the understated beauty of this hand roll. The "wow" appeal is in the taste. The Japanese Omelette offers sweet and savory flavors, while little bursts of heat pop across the tongue from the Wasabi Faux Roe. Nutty sesame seeds complement and enhance the fragrant shiso. If you prefer more sweetness, use Vegetarian Eel Sauce (page 26) for dipping in lieu of soy sauce.

Rice Prep Time: Up to 1½ hours
Sushi Prep Time: 10 minutes
Makes 4 rolls

Four 4 x 7-in (10 x 18-cm) nori sheets
1 cup (200 g) Traditional Sushi Rice, Brown Sushi Rice, Quinoa Sushi "Rice" or Multi-Grain Sushi Rice (pages 21–23)
4 Japanese Omelette Sheets (page 66), cut into thin strips
4 teaspoons toasted sesame seeds
8 large shiso (perilla) or basil leaves
4 teaspoons Wasabi Faux Roe (page 68)

Align 1 sheet of nori across your left palm with the rough side facing up. Press 4 tablespoons of the sushi rice on the left third of the nori.

Sprinkle 1 teaspoon of the sesame seeds over the rice. Arrange 2 large shiso or basil leaves down the center of the rice. Add ¼ of the omelette strips and 1 teaspoon of the Wasabi Faux Roe.

Take the bottom left corner of the nori and fold it over the fillings until it reaches the top point just beyond the rice. Roll downward, forming a tight cone, until all the nori has been wrapped around. If desired, secure the loose edge with a single grain of rice.

Repeat steps with the remaining ingredients to make 3 more rolls. Serve immediately.

Hold nori and spread 4 Tbsp rice on the left third.

Arrange fillings down the center of the rice.

Roll into a cone.

# Tempura Avocado Hand Rolls

Traditionally, when tempura dipping sauce is served, it is accompanied by small mounds of freshly grated ginger root and daikon radish. This can be messy when trying to dip a hand roll, so here a bit of each is spread across the sushi rice before the cone is rolled.

**Rice Prep Time: Up to 1½ hours**
**Sushi Prep Time: 15 minutes**
**Makes 4 rolls**

Oil for frying
1 avocado, cut into 8 wedges
Potato starch or cornstarch (corn flour) for dusting
½ cup (125 ml) Vegan Tempura Batter (page 34)
Four 4 x 7-in (10 x 18-cm) nori sheets
1 cup (200 g) Traditional Sushi Rice, Brown Sushi Rice, Quinoa Sushi "Rice" or Multi-Grain Sushi Rice (pages 21–23)
2 teaspoons grated daikon radish
2 teaspoons grated fresh ginger root
1 large romaine lettuce leaf, cut into thin strips
One 4-in (10-cm) cucumber length, cut into matchsticks
Tempura Dipping Sauce (page 26)

Heat at least 1 in (2.5 cm) of oil in a skillet to 350°F (175°C).

Dust the avocado wedges with potato starch, then dip in the Vegan Tempura Batter. Add to the hot oil. Pour 1 tablespoon of tempura batter over the top of the oil after adding the avocado. Fry until the batter is golden brown, about 2 minutes. Drain avocado wedges on a wire rack.

Align 1 sheet of nori across your left palm with the rough side facing up. Press 4 tablespoons of the sushi rice on the left third of the nori.

Smear ½ teaspoon of the grated daikon and ½ teaspoon of the grated ginger down the center of the rice. Add ¼ of the romaine lettuce. Top with 2 of the tempura avocado pieces. If you have crunchy tempura bits, sprinkle those on top, too! Add ¼ of the cucumber matchsticks.

Take the bottom left corner of the nori and fold it over the fillings until it reaches the top point just beyond the rice. Roll downward, forming a tight cone, until all the nori has been wrapped around. Secure the loose edge with a single grain of rice.

Repeat steps with remaining ingredients to make 3 more rolls. Serve immediately.

# Natto and Scallion Hand Rolls

*Natto* is made of soybeans fermented with the healthy bacteria *Bactilus subtilus*. During the fermentation process, it develops a pungent smell similar to that of "stinky" cheeses. The fermentation process produces a thin layer of "slime" over the beans, which gets stringy upon stirring. Handling natto can be messy. Try dipping 2 metal spoons in cold water right before scooping up the natto—just as you would dip your fingers before handling sushi rice. Use one spoon to scoop up the natto and the other to tame flyaways.

**Rice Prep Time: Up to 1½ hours**
**Sushi Prep Time: 15 minutes**
**Makes 4 rolls**

Four 4 x 7-in (10 x 18-cm) nori sheets
1 cup (200 g) Traditional Sushi Rice, Brown Sushi Rice, Quinoa Sushi "Rice" or Multi-Grain Sushi Rice (pages 21-23)
4 teaspoons Sesame Soy Mustard (page 29)

4 oz (115 g) natto
2 green onions (scallions), thinly sliced
4 teaspoons Basic Furikake Seasoning (page 30)

Align 1 sheet of nori across your left palm with the rough side facing up. Press 4 tablespoons of the sushi rice on the left third of the nori.

Spread 1 teaspoon of the Sesame Soy Mustard down the center of the rice.

Add ¼ of the natto. Top with ¼ of the green onions. Sprinkle with furikake.

Take the bottom left corner of the nori and fold it over the fillings until it reaches the top point just beyond the rice. Roll downward, forming a tight cone, until all the nori has been wrapped around. If desired, secure the loose edge with a single grain of rice.

Repeat steps to make 3 more rolls. Serve immediately.

Press 4 Tbsp rice on the nori sheet.

Spread Sesame Soy Mustard on rice.

Use wet spoons to add the natto.

# Chapter 8

# DESSERTS & DRINKS

Though dessert is the ending of a meal, I often think of it first when planning a menu. A meal well done deserves a sweet reward, and a sushi meal is no different. You'll find that while most of these desserts are not typical Japanese sweets, their flavors pair quite well with ingredients used throughout other chapters. Some of the pantry staples used—such as Japanese breadcrumbs—do double duty, both as reference to relevant flavors and as practical shortcuts that lead to a delicious end.

What to drink with sushi is a question that often yields the same answers: beer and sake. Both, of course, are great sidekicks, but even those standards can use a little upgrade to enhance the overall sushi experience. Using the same approach as for the desserts, drinks can be tailored to suit the flavors of what is being served. Chilled Sake with Vegetable-Flavored Salts is a refreshing way to enjoy sake that isn't sweet. If a non-alcoholic drink suits your mood, try Iced Green Tea or Pomegranate Ginger Fizzy.

# Almond Crème Brownies

**The aroma** of almonds fills these brownies. If you can, avoid cutting them until they are completely cool, or they will fall apart. If the temptation is too much to resist, serve them warm in a bowl with a spoon. They will still be a bit gooey, albeit delicious.

**Prep Time:** 15 minutes
**Cook Time:** 25 minutes
**Makes about 8 servings**

½ cup (250 g) butter, plus more
 for greasing pan
2 oz (60 g) semisweet chocolate
 chips
¾ cup (150 g) sugar
2 eggs plus one egg yolk
1 teaspoon vanilla extract
½ teaspoon almond extract
¾ cup (100 g) all-purpose flour
½ cup (40 g) slivered almonds

**Almond Crème**
1 cup (125 g) confectioners' sugar
1 cup (125 g) almond flour
1 egg white
1 teaspoon almond extract
1 tablespoon heavy cream
Pinch of salt

Grease an 8-in (20-cm) square baking pan with butter. Heat oven to 350°F (175°C).

Place the butter in a saucepan over medium heat and stir until melted. Remove from heat and stir in the chocolate chips. Set aside to cool.

In a medium bowl, lightly beat the sugar, eggs, egg yolk, vanilla extract and almond extract. Add the melted chocolate mixture and the flour. Stir until mixture is consistent. Pour batter into the greased baking pan.

Prepare the Almond Crème: Place the confectioners' sugar, almond flour, egg white, almond extract, heavy cream and salt in a food processor. Process for several seconds, or until mixture is combined.

Spoon the Almond Crème over the batter and swirl it into the batter with a spatula or spoon. Sprinkle the slivered almonds over the top.

Bake for 25 minutes, or until brownies are set in the middle. Cool completely before cutting.

# Chilled Sake with Vegetable-Flavored Salts

Working with fresh vegetable peels will yield great results, but peels that have been in the refrigerator overnight yield even better results. The refrigerator starts the process of dehydrating the peels and decreases oven time. Serving premium chilled sake with these salts brings out the natural sweetness of the sake. Try using them as finishing salt for cold dishes, too.

Cook Time: 45 minutes to 1 hour
Prep Time: 10 minutes, plus sake
chilling time

**Red Bell Pepper Salt**
Peel of 1 red bell pepper
1 cup (290 g) coarse salt

**Cucumber Salt**
Peel of 1 cucumber
1 cup (290 g) coarse salt

**Butternut Squash Salt**
3 oz (85 g) butternut squash,
   peeled and shaved thin
1 cup (290 g) coarse salt

**Premium sake, to taste**

Place individual vegetable peels in separate bowls. Cover each type of peel with 1 cup of salt. Keeping types separate, place the peel and salt in a food processor. Pulse to break up.

Prepare separate lined baking sheets. Spread one type of vegetable salt in a very thin layer on each. Preheat oven to 200°F (95°C). Bake salts for 45 minutes to an hour, or until very dry. Allow to cool completely before using.

To serve, pour the sake into a ceramic serving pitcher and nestle it into a bowl of ice. Provide vegetable salts on the side. Take a sip of sake and follow it with a small pinch of flavored salt.

Set peels in bowls and cover with salt.

Process peels and salt into small bits.

Toss mixture several times to combine.

Spread salt onto lined baking sheet.

# Fruit-Filled Mochi Balls

Strawberries are a simple choice for this fun dessert, but many other types of fruits will yield delicious results. Berries and stone fruits such as peaches, plums and apricots work nicely. For the best-looking end result, select berries that are similar in size or use a melon baller to create uniform portions of fruit.

Prep Time: 25 minutes
Cook Time: 3 minutes
Makes 12 pieces

¾ cup (100 g) glutinous rice flour (*mochiko*)
¾ cup (185 ml) water
1 drop yellow, green or red food coloring (optional)
4 tablespoons sugar
Confectioners' sugar for dusting
3 oz (85 g) red bean paste (*anko*)
12 pieces of fruit such as strawberries, peaches, plums or apricots

In a microwave-safe bowl, mix the rice flour, water, food coloring (if using) and sugar. Cover loosely with plastic wrap and microwave on high for 2 minutes. Stir again with a whisk and return to the microwave for 2 minutes more. Handle carefully—the mochi will be extremely hot.

Dust your work surface generously with confectioners' sugar. Place the cooked mochi dough on top and allow to sit until cool enough to handle.

Roll the dough to about ¼ in (.75 cm) thick. Dust the rolling pin with additional confectioners' sugar to prevent sticking.

Cut 12 circles out of the dough using a 3-in (7.5-cm) round cookie cutter. (If needed, pinch together dough scraps and re-roll.) Wipe excess confectioners' sugar from one side of the mochi using a pastry brush or clean towel.

Roll a piece of fruit in about 1 tablespoon of the red bean paste, working to cover it completely. Place the bean-paste-covered fruit inside the mochi dough and pinch closed. Place pinched side down on the dusted work surface and twist several times to shape. Repeat with remaining mochi and fillings.

## Variation
### Cherry Almond Mochi

Remove the pits and stems from 12 cherries. Place in a small bowl with 4 tablespoons of sake. Cook, roll and cut the dough as directed. Substitute almond paste for the red bean paste. Drain cherries and pat dry. Use 1 cherry per mochi circle. Wrap and shape as directed.

Stir dough ingredients in a microwave-safe bowl.

Drop the dough onto a sugar-dusted surface.

Roll dough into a thin sheet.

Cut dough into 3-in (7.5-cm) circles.

Wrap paste-covered fruit balls in dough circles.

Roll the mochi ball to seal edges.

# Iced Green Tea

**Good iced green tea starts with a good green tea bag. A bold variety such as sencha produces the best result. If you like a stronger flavor, gently squeeze the tea bags over the pitcher before discarding them.**

**Prep Time: 15 minutes**
**Makes about 6 servings**

4 cups (1 liter) warm water
10 green tea bags

**Lemon-Ginger Syrup**
½ cup (125 ml) water
One ½-in (13-mm) length
  fresh ginger root, peeled
  and roughly chopped
½ cup (100 g) sugar
Juice of 1 lemon
Lemon slices, for garnish

Place the 4 cups warm water in a non-metal serving pitcher. Wrap the strings of the tea bags around a chopstick and suspend them over the pitcher. Dunk the tea bags a few times to "activate" them. Allow to steep for 15 minutes. Remove the tea bags and squeeze the liquid from them into the pitcher before discarding. Chill tea before serving.

Make the Lemon-Ginger Syrup: Bring the ½ cup water and fresh ginger root to a boil. Remove from heat, cover and steep for 5 minutes. Remove ginger root. Return water to heat and add sugar, stirring well to dissolve. Simmer for 5 minutes. Stir in lemon juice and cool completely before using.

To serve the tea, fill a glass with ice cubes and add desired amount of tea. Sweeten to taste with Lemon-Ginger Syrup. Garnish with a lemon slice.

# Green Tea Ice Cream

**Sweetened condensed milk doesn't get the credit it deserves. Thanks to its fat content, using it in ice cream makes for speedy, no-fuss deliciousness. Be sure that the heavy cream is very cold for best results.**

**Prep Time: 10 minutes**
**Freezing Time: 2 to 6 hours**
**Makes about 1 pint (475 ml)**

2 tablespoons matcha
  (green tea powder)
2 cups (500 ml) heavy cream
One 14-oz (415-ml) can
  sweetened condensed milk
1-2 drops green food
  coloring, optional
2 teaspoons vanilla extract

In a large bowl, whisk the matcha powder into the heavy cream. Get rid of as many lumps as possible. Using a mixer on high speed, beat the heavy cream until stiff peaks begin to form, about 2–3 minutes.

In a separate bowl, stir together the sweetened condensed milk, food coloring (if using) and vanilla extract. Gently fold into the whipped cream mixture. Continue folding until the mixture is combined, being careful not to completely deflate the whipped cream.

Pour the mixture into the reservoir of an ice-cream maker and freeze according to manufacturer's directions. Once finished, the ice cream will be very soft. Transfer to a freezer-safe container and freeze for another 2 hours before serving.

To freeze without an ice cream maker, line a metal loaf pan with plastic wrap. Spread mixture into the pan and lay a piece of plastic wrap directly on top. Freeze for at least 6 hours before enjoying.

# Fruit Tartlets

True to its name, the puff pastry will rise to several times its original thickness during the cooking process. This is okay, as it can be poked and deflated. One bite into the creamy center down through the flaky, crunchy crust, though, and you won't mind the minor inconvenience.

Prep Time: 10 minutes
Cook Time: 25 minutes
Makes 12 tartlets

Butter for greasing pan
2 sheets frozen puff pastry, thawed
One 14-oz (415-ml) can sweetened condensed milk
3 egg yolks
4 tablespoons fresh lime juice
1 teaspoon lime zest
½ cup (125 g) apricot jam
1 teaspoon grated fresh ginger
2 cups (350 g) assorted fresh fruit

Preheat oven to 350°F (175°C). Butter a standard 12-cup muffin tin. Set aside.

Using a 3-in (8-cm) round cutter, cut 12 rounds out of the puff pastry. Prick each round several times with a fork. Press the rounds into the cavities of the muffin tin.

Bake for 15 minutes or until the puff pastry begins to turn golden brown.

Remove from oven and use the back of a large spoon to deflate the centers of the puff pastry. Allow to cool.

In a medium bowl, mix the sweetened condensed milk, egg yolks, lime juice and lime zest.

Pour into the cooled pastry shells and bake for 10 minutes, or until filling is set.

Remove tarts from the muffin tin and cool completely. Heat the apricot jam in a microwave-safe bowl for 15 seconds. Stir in the grated ginger. Spoon the apricot jam mixture over the tops of the tarts, reserving some for the final presentation.

Distribute the fresh fruit equally among the tarts. Use a pastry brush to brush the remaining apricot jam mixture on top.

Keep refrigerated until ready to serve. Before serving, add a dollop of Ginger Whipped Cream, to taste.

## Ginger Whipped Cream

1 cup (250 ml) chilled heavy cream
3 tablespoons confectioners' sugar
1 teaspoon vanilla extract
1 teaspoon powdered ginger

Place heavy cream, confectioners' sugar, vanilla extract, and powdered ginger in a medium bowl. Beat until soft peaks form. Serve immediately.

# Pomegranate Ginger Fizzy

I like to have a little something fizzy when enjoying sushi. This drink is like a fruity soda, but isn't overly sweet. The addition of sake and bitters can easily transform it into a cocktail.

Prep Time: 5 minutes
Makes 4 servings

½ cup (125 ml) Lemon-Ginger Syrup (page 122)
½ cup (125 ml) pomegranate juice
½ cup (125 ml) mango nectar
Club soda, to taste

Combine the Lemon-Ginger Syrup, pomegranate juice, and mango nectar in a pitcher. Chill.

To serve, fill four glasses with ice. Fill each glass ¾ full of pomegranate mixture, then top off with club soda. Stir well and serve.

## Variation
### Sake Pomegranate Ginger Fizzy
Prepare the Lemon-Ginger Syrup and pomegranate mixture. To serve, place 1 sugar cube and 1 dash of orange-flavored bitters in a glass. Combine 1½ oz (45 ml) sake and 3 oz (90 ml) of the pomegranite-ginger mixture with ice in a cocktail shaker. Shake well and strain into glass. Top with a splash of club soda.

# Sake Salty Dog

The addition of yuzu juice, from a Japanese citrus fruit with a distinctive flavor, and sake makes this cocktail something special. If yuzu juice is not available, use all grapefruit juice. If you're feeling brave, use Cucumber Salt, Butternut Squash Salt or Red Bell Pepper Salt (page 119) instead of kosher salt to rim each glass.

Prep Time: 5 minutes
Makes 2 cocktails

2 slices grapefruit
Kosher salt, for rims of glasses
2 teaspoons sugar
½ cup (125 ml) sake
4 tablespoons yuzu juice
½ cup (125 ml) grapefruit juice

Run a grapefruit slice around the rim of a highball glass. Repeat on a second glass with a second grapefruit slice. Dip rims into kosher salt. If desired, reserve the grapefruit slices as garnish.

Place 1 teaspoon of sugar in the bottom of each glass. Add 4 tablespoons of sake to each glass and muddle. Fill each glass with ice. Add 2 tablespoons yuzu juice and 4 tablespoons grapefruit juice to each glass. Stir well before serving.

# Panko Fruit Crisp

Mix and match your favorite fruits for this simple dessert. For best results, use stone fruits such as cherries, peaches, nectarines and plums; berries, apples or pears are also great. If desired, serve warm with a scoop of good vanilla ice cream or Ginger Whipped Cream (page 123).

**Cook Time: 35–40 minutes**
**Makes 6–8 servings**

4 cups (700 g) sliced fruit of your choice, peeled, cored or pitted, and sliced
Juice of 1 lemon
1 cup (200 g) sugar
3 tablespoons potato starch or cornstarch (corn flour)
1 teaspoon grated fresh ginger root
1 cup (65 g) *panko* breadcrumbs
½ cup (65 g) all-purpose flour
½ cup (100 g) brown sugar
½ cup unsalted butter, melted
Pinch of salt

Preheat oven to 375°F (190°C).

Lightly butter a 9-in (23-cm) square glass or ceramic baking dish. Pour in the prepared fruit and add the lemon juice, sugar, potato starch and grated ginger. Toss to mix well.

In a bowl, combine the panko, all-purpose flour, brown sugar, melted butter and salt. The mixture should be crumbly. Distribute evenly over top of the fruit.

Bake for 35–40 minutes, or until the fruit begins to visibly bubble.

Serve hot or warm. Leftovers may be stored in the refrigerator for up to 3 days.

# Index

# About Tuttle
## "Books to Span the East and West"

Our core mission at Tuttle Publishing is to create books which bring people together one page at a time. Tuttle was founded in 1832 in the small New England town of Rutland, Vermont (USA). Our fundamental values remain as strong today as they were then—to publish best-in-class books informing the English-speaking world about the countries and peoples of Asia. The world has become a smaller place today and Asia's economic, cultural and political influence has expanded, yet the need for meaningful dialogue and information about this diverse region has never been greater. Since 1948, Tuttle has been a leader in publishing books on the cultures, arts, cuisines, languages and literatures of Asia. Our authors and photographers have won numerous awards and Tuttle has published thousands of books on subjects ranging from martial arts to paper crafts. We welcome you to explore the wealth of information available on Asia at www.tuttlepublishing.com.

## Acknowledgment

Raise a glass for my dearest Stan, who endured yet another many months of the "lovely" mixed smell of rice vinegar and freshly brewed coffee each morning. L'Chaim!

Published by Tuttle Publishing, an imprint of Periplus Editions (HK) Ltd.

www.tuttlepublishing.com

Copyright © 2016 Marisa Baggett

Library of Congress Cataloging-in-Publication Data
Names: Baggett, Marisa, author.
Title: Vegetarian sushi secrets : 101 healthy and delicious recipes / Marisa Baggett.
Description: Tokyo ; Rutland, Vermont : Tuttle Publishing, [2016] | Includes index.
Identifiers: LCCN 2016006660 | ISBN 9784805313701 (pbk.)
Subjects: LCSH: Sushi. | Cooking, Japanese. | Vegetarian cooking. | LCGFT: Cookbooks.
Classification: LCC TX724.5.J3 B3423 2016 | DDC 641.5952--dc23 LC record available at https://lccn.loc.gov/2016006660

ISBN: 978-4-8053-1370-1

North America, Latin America & Europe
Tuttle Publishing
364 Innovation Drive
North Clarendon, VT 05759-9436 U.S.A.
Tel: (802) 773-8930; Fax: (802) 773-6993
info@tuttlepublishing.com; www.tuttlepublishing.com

Japan
Tuttle Publishing
Yaekari Building, 3rd Floor
5-4-12 Osaki, Shinagawa-ku, Tokyo 141 0032
Tel: (81) 3 5437-0171; Fax: (81) 3 5437-0755
sales@tuttle.co.jp; www.tuttle.co.jp

Asia Pacific
Berkeley Books Pte. Ltd.
61 Tai Seng Avenue #02-12, Singapore 534167
Tel: (65) 6280-1330; Fax: (65) 6280-6290
inquiries@periplus.com.sg; www.periplus.com

20 19 18 17 16          5 4 3 2 1

Printed in China 1607RR

TUTTLE PUBLISHING® is a registered trademark of Tuttle Publishing, a division of Periplus Editions (HK) Ltd.